C000019210

THE END OF AN ERA

The Story of the 1950 Rugby League Tour

CONTENTS

Acknowledgements

Bibliography

Introduction

Chapter One
(Controversy over selection mars the tour start)

Chapter Two
(The Aussie critics are suitably impressed with the Englishmen)

Chapter Three
(Trouble with referees, injuries and a game cancelled but tourists are unbeaten in NSW)

Chapter Four
(Tour derailed, Test match lost, manager in trouble)

Chapter Five
(Return to NSW Ashes lost)

Chapter Six
(NZ two Tests lost a player home early)

Chapter Seven
(Home to face the music – whitewash claims)

Pen Pictures

Games played on Tour

ACKNOWLEDGEMENTS

There are many reasons just why a book such as this gets written, it could simply be the writer is interested enough in a topic to sit at a computer and write about it. On the other hand, it could be a chance comment or remark that attracts the writers' interest. Having written a series of books covering the tours down under by the Rugby League between the two World Wars, I felt that was enough. However, a number of people pointed out the obvious gap in the series. The 1946 tour has been very well covered in a book 'The Indomitables'. I had covered the 1954 tour but nothing had been written of the 1950 tour, hence the gap.

I began to do a little research and found there was a good deal of controversy involved on that tour both on and off the field that sparked my interest. The end result is this book. As ever there are many people to thank in getting this book written. Terry Williams the former Historian at the NRL Museum at Moore Park in Sydney was as ever a font of information which he willingly shared with me. He also very kindly provided a number of illustrations reproduced in the book. As the newspaper coverage of the New Zealand leg of the tour was at best sketchy, I am indebted to John Coffey who once again was also a mine of information. He supplied many newspaper cutting of the games played in that country.

To those reporters who covered events on and off the field all those years ago also deserve my thanks, they covered some torrid events on that tour with clarity and honesty. I hope that comes through in the book. To all those players who participated in the tour both Australian and New Zealanders along with the British tourists go my thanks for without them there would be no book.

Finally, to my wife Janet for once more proof reading, correcting and suggesting additions to the manuscript my heartfelt thanks.

BIBLIOGRAPHY

The following newspapers were referred to in the book.

Australia:-

The Arrow, Brisbane Courier, Cootamundra Times, The Daily Standard (Queensland), The Daily News (Perth), Evening News (Sydney), Morning Bulletin (Rockhampton), Newcastle Morning Herald, Newcastle Sun, Northern Star Lismore), Referee, Riverina Grazier, The Sun, Sunday Sun, Sunday Herald, The Telegraph (Brisbane), Sunday Times, Sydney Mail, Sydney Morning Herald, Sydney Sportsman, Western Champion.

New Zealand:-

Auckland Star, Auckland Herald, Evening Post (Wellington), Ellesmere Guardian (Canterbury), Otago Daily Times, Press (Canterbury).

Books referred to:-

Gone North Volume 1 and 2 by Robert Gate, The struggle for the Ashes, by Robert Gate, The Best in the Northern Union, The Rugby League Lions by Les Hoole, The Lions Roar Again, Northern Lions on Tour all by Tom Mather. The Ashes Trophy Tour by Tom Mather, A Century of Rugby League 1908-2008 by Ian Heads and David Middleton.

INTRODUCTION

With the second World War now a slowly fading memory the international rugby league scene was seemingly back to normality. The tour to Australia in 1946 had been very successful and visits to England by both Australia and New Zealand had seen similar success on the field. There was a growing believe or should that be complacency within the game with not only supporters but also administrators that nothing would change. The Ashes were exactly where they belonged, in the hands of the British. A series win against New Zealand was also achieved albeit by a two to one margin. What could go wrong?

It was in this atmosphere that the 1949-50 season commenced with all in the game knowing that at its end a team was to tour down under. It was the ninth such tour and all in the game expected it would end in the same manner as previous tours. The series in Australia would be tough but the Englishmen would win through and return with the Ashes after all they had held them for the best part of thirty years. As the season had progressed so had the excitement as to just who would be entrusted to retain the Ashes and who would manage the touring party. These were the questions on everyone's lips.

The tour party was finally announced and with it came the usual controversy over who had or had not been selected. What no one knew at that time was just how tumultuous this ninth tour would turn out to be both on and off the field. It was a tour that would see:-

* The Ashes lost for the first time in thirty years.
* Selection controversies for the tour rock the game itself.
* The first NSW leg of the tour see the tourists undefeated.
* The first Test won but played in awful conditions.
* Controversy raise its head over referees in Queensland.
* The second Test lost with two English players sent off.
* Manager and players in trouble for comments made about the official in the second Test.
* The RFL state that on future tours players would not be allowed to write for newspapers.
* Claims the two tour managers were at odds with each other on the tour.
* Claims that one of the managers missed a number of games and functions.
* Player dissatisfaction of team selection and claims of Test favourites.
* The third Test lost in playing conditions worse that those of the first Test.
* Two of the players return home early.
* The four wingmen selected suffer problems all through the tour.
* Two Tests lost in New Zealand.
* The English team lose four consecutive Test matches for the first time ever.

* A whitewash by the Rugby League of the managerial problems.

The book traces the activities both on and off the field of this momentous tour that really did prove to be the End of An Era for the English game. Gone for ever was the total domination of the game by the Rugby League that had spanned thirty years. It was a domination that would not be seen again until the Australian domination of the game began in the early seventies and continues to this day.

THE END OF AN ERA
The Story of the 1950 Rugby League Tour

CHAPTER ONE
(Controversy over selection mars the tour start)

As 1949 came along in the United Kingdom everything in the rugby league world in the country was rosy. When the war had come to an end the Rugby League Council had moved quickly to re-establish the game on an international level. The 1946 tour to Australia and New Zealand had been organized, not without difficulties. The Government realizing the country needed to get back to normal once the conflict came to an end were extremely helpful. They had allowed the tourists in 1946 to sail down under in the aircraft carrier Indomitable.

That tour had seen the Englishmen return undefeated in the Test matches in Australia. While it was true the first Test played at the Sydney Cricket Ground had been a close-run affair the end result was a draw, at eight points each. The second and third Test matches had seen the tourists come away with two victories 14-5 in the second and 20-7 in the third. The results in New Zealand were not unexpected after a long tour the one and only Test match being lost 13-8.

On the reciprocal tour which had come to an end in England at the end of January the game had finished on an international high. For only the second time the Test series had resulted in a three to nil whitewash to the home side. Prior to that the New Zealand players had toured the country and they also had been defeated two to one. The feeling within the game was that the ravages of the war had been mastered and the game was as strong now as it had ever been. It was against this background that planning could begin for the 1950 tour back to Australia and New Zealand.

Certainly, the feeling was that all was right with the world. The King, George the Sixth was still on the throne and as popular as ever. The Olympic games held in the capital city had proved to be the great success no one really predicted. In the game the Ashes had been retained in truth it was thirty years since the trophy, such as it was, had been left down in Sydney way back in 1920. As planning got under way no one really considered the possibility that the Ashes would not be retain once more. After all the playing strength was as good now as it had ever been in the history of the game.

The planning for the tour was seemingly a straight forward affair after all it was to be the ninth such tour to be undertaken. Passage would be booked for the players to travel out by sea as always. Playing strip would be decided upon and ordered as would the necessary playing kit shin pads, shoulder pads and the likes. The only problem as was always the case was selecting the players who would make up the tour party. In order that selection was seen as fair and transparent a committee of twelve men would be handed that responsibility.

At this stage it must be pointed out that even the planning stage of the tour was not without its controversial incident. As had always been the case members of the Rugby League were asked to apply for the positions of tour managers. In truth there was normally only one position available as one manager from the previous tour seems to have been selected for a second tour. The reasoning being that having been on tour they were aware of the problems down under. Also, it was very likely they would have made contacts in Australia that they could use once in the country.

So, it was that at a Council meeting there were seven people who had applied for the managers jobs. They were Tom Brown from Wigan, Bob Anderton from Warrington a former two tour manager. M.W. Gabbitt from Barrow along with A. Berry from Featherstone and W.A. Cockcroft of Hull K.R. Added to the mix was George Oldroyd the Dewsbury Chairman and finally Tom Spedding the Belle Vue Rangers Secretary. All expected that Brown and Anderton would gain selection but that proved not to be the case.

To the surprise of many in the game Oldroyd and Spedding were appointed. With hindsight it was a decision that would have disastrous consequences for all in the game. George Oldroyd was a forty seven year old Yorkshire Mill owner with interests in Ireland and the horse racing fraternity He was the Chairman of the Dewsbury club and while on the Council he was also Chairman of the Finance Committee. He was used to getting his own way and preferred the big stick rather than the carrot approach to dealing with people.

Tom Spedding on the other hand had only been on Council for a year or so. He had been the manager of a hotel on the Isle of Man before taking over running the entertainment complex that was Belle Vue. He was also the secretary of the Belle Vue Rangers club which he told people was his 'hobby'. Being in the entertainment industry he was used to a carrot approach to placating people the opposite to Oldroyd. As we shall see later the combination proved a disaster in Australia in general and Queensland in particular.

As is ever the case as that 1949-50 season began speculation commenced in all quarters as to who was worthy of a place on the tour and who was not. The twelve apostles that made up the selection committee also formed their own opinions. As we know a camel is a horse designed by a committee and so that maxim proved to be true when selecting the best twenty-six players to travel down under. The problem was that players whom certain selectors favoured were simply not playing well as the season progressed. On the other hand, a number of unfavoured players were actually performing so well that they had to come into consideration.

The speculation all came to a head on the 1st March 1950 when the international match between England and Wales was scheduled to be played at Central Park

Wigan. The press had been informed that following the game the selectors would meet to finalize the squad that was to make the trip. It must be remembered that players were still going to be away from home for a considerable length of time so selectors would have to assume players could or would get time off from their employers. From the press release it could be assumed that the majority of the party had already been penciled in and it was simply a matter of dotting the I's and crossing the T's.

The problems arose following what turned out to be a very dull and uninspiring game which saw England scrape home by 11-6. The only bright spot in the whole afternoon was the performance of the Wigan wingman Jack Hilton. He seemed to revel in the confines of his home ground and scored all three of the English tries. Given that had not appeared to figure in the minds of the selectors his performance caused them great consternation. When the twelve selectors sat down players who had been a shoo in prior to the game were now being hotly debated in committee. Other players who had been on the fringes suddenly were thrust well and truly into the mix. Also dare we say it certain selectors favoured Yorkshire players while others looked to Lancashire players.

Following the game, the press eagerly awaited the announcement from the selection committee. They waited and they waited and at midnight they were told that the committee had not finished its deliberations and would reconvene on the following day. They also informed the reporters that the squad would be released to the press on Friday the 3rd March. When they did release the names, they were subjected to a barrage of criticism from all quarters. The press, supporters and club officials all had their say on the team.

The twenty-six players who were to travel down to Australia and New Zealand were:-

Fullbacks: M. Ryan (Wigan) J. Ledgard (Leigh)
Wingers: A. Daniels (Halifax) R. Pollard (Dewsbury)
L. Williams (Hunslet) J. Hilton (Wigan)
Centres: E. Ward (Bradford Northern Captain) E.
Ashcroft (Wigan) J. Cunliffe (Wigan) T. Danby
(Salford)
Stand-Off: W. Horne (Barrow) R. Williams (Leeds)
Scrum Half: T. Bradshaw (Wigan) A Pepperell
(Workington Town)
Hooker: J. Egan (Wigan) F. Osmond (Swinton)
Prop Forward:- K. Gee (Wigan) J. Featherstone
(Warrington) F. Higgins (Widnes) E Gwyther (Belle
Vue Rangers)
Second Row: D. Phillips (Belle Vue Rangers) H.
Murphy (Wakefield Trinity) R. Naughton (Widnes)
R. Ryan (Warrington)
Loose Forward: K. Traill (Bradford Northern) H.
Street (Dewsbury)

No sooner was the public aware of the squad than the outrage began and the major target of all the anger was the none selection of Dave Valentine the Huddersfield loose forward. He had been injured and the selectors felt that his form coming into the selection period did not warrant his inclusion. Many pointed out that other players were equally as guilty of that crime but they had gained selection. The criticism did not stop there and it was not only the press that were having their say either.

Tom Brown who was a former Chairman of the Rugby League stated that **"The omission of Valentine, the greatest lock-forward in the game is a staggering blunder. Another stupid mistake was leaving out George Curran who with Egan and Gee made up one of the finest front rows in the history of the game."**

The great Australian forward Arthur Clues who at the time was playing for Leeds added his two penny-worth:

"I am dumbfounded at the omission of Valentine, he is a forward in a thousand whose great play helped England win every Test in 1948."

Clues was joined in those sentiments by the other Australian great Huddersfield winger Lionel Cooper.

It was not just the none selection of Valentine that upset folks either. The great ex-Saint Helens wingman Alf Ellaby said of the selection: **"There has never been a bigger mistake than the omission of Wigan wingman Gordon Ratcliffe. He is the most dangerous back in Britain. The inclusion of Hilton in preference to Radcliffe is blatantly inconsistent with current form."**

Ellaby was not done with his criticism and went much further than others perhaps felt was prudent: **"It is obvious the committee let prejudice come in when the dropped Valentine, generally regarded as a 100 to 1 certainty."**

There was one selection that most were agreed upon as really being controversial and that was the Salford centre Tom Danby. Danby was in his first season in Rugby League and many felt that while he had played well in the trial game at Wigan the selectors had placed too much emphasis on that rather than going for a more experienced player who would perhaps cope better in Australian conditions. Danby was no stranger to top level rugby albeit in the other code. In January 1949 he had represented England against Wales before throwing in his lot with Salford. Not only that but when the Australian rugby union team toured England in 1948 Danby played against them on two occasions. Still many felt he was a little too inexperienced for such a tour.

There was another player who was literally in his first season in the game at the top level and that was the Dewsbury wingman Roy Pollard. He was just twenty-three when selected to go on tour but boy did he come from cracking stock! His father was Charles Pollard the former Wakefield player who had gone on tour in 1920. His uncle was Ernest Pollard who had also gone on tour in 1932. The press were a little less reticent of Pollard given his obvious pedigree in the game.

Many also questioned why Jack Hilton had been preferred to the other Wigan wingman Ratcliffe. Hilton had begun his career with Salford and proved to be a try scorer par excellent. In one game against Leigh he would cross for six tries was it any wonder his home town club were keen to get him back. During the war he served in North Africa and during the height of battle he was struck by two pieces of shrapnel. One hit him in the wrist the other in the thigh. Luckily, they were not to affect his sporting ability and on joining Wigan he won every honour the game had to offer. He was considered to be the fastest wingman in the game at the time hence his selection for the tour.

It was left to the Chairman of the Rugby League, Harry Hornby, who was also the chairman of the selection committee to try to answer the mounting criticism of their selections:

"This team is not everyone's cup of tea but despite the adverse criticism the committee is standing by its choice."

In truth he could say nothing else other than defend himself and his other selectors. As we shall see later events actually were to in some small way justify some of the selections.

If the feeling was that the criticism would fade away sadly it did not. Just a couple of days later reporters had to seek clarification from the Secretary of the League, Bill Fallowfield, with regard to one of those selected. Albert Pepperell the Workington scrum half was one of three Cumbrian brothers in the game and many reporters felt the wrong initial had been released. They thought the player actually selected was his brother Russell Pepperell from the Huddersfield club. Reporters in Yorkshire were unanimous in their opinion that Russell was a better player and they felt he should have been in the squad instead of Jack Cunliffe who they said had spent the last ten years as a reserve in the Wigan club.

The Yorkshire reporters also to a man were staggered at the exclusion of Valentine. Perhaps they had a point as the League Champions at the time were the Huddersfield club and they had not one player in the touring party. It was all very messy and the blame could be squarely laid at the Council's door. After all it was they who had approved a twelve-man committee and as we know in the game of rugby league it is difficult to get two people to agree let alone a dozen!

Others were to question the selection of both Doug Phillips and Gwyther as neither of them had been playing well enough to make the Welsh team that had lost to England in the recent trial game. None the less they had made the squad. The Warrington second row Ryan had not been in any reporters top one hundred to make selection a month prior to getting the nod. Ken Traill came in for attention also as many felt there were better loose forwards and they were playing better but had not come into the reckoning.

In actual fact there was a great deal of substance to the criticisms made. When the Australians had toured in 1948-49 the home side had won the series three nil and yet nine of those players who had achieved this were not selected to tour. Foster, Valentine, Owens, White, Curran, from the forwards had been discarded while Pimblett, Lawrenson, Helme and McCormack in the backs had faced the axe also. It is difficult to believe that in the space of one season such experienced internationals should all suffer a loss of form to such a level as to rule them out of contention.

Just two weeks later one criticism was laid to rest when Les Williams the Hunslet wingman withdrew from the tour. Sadly, Williams had been unable to secure time off from sitting his final examinations at Leeds Carnegie College until after his return from Australia. The selectors immediately called in Gordon Ratcliffe the Wigan flyer as his replacement. The selection committee had further headaches as the departure day of the 20th April fast approached. Willie Horne the mercurial Barrow stand off had broken a finger and it was a race to ensure he was fit to go aboard the Himalaya that was to take them down under. The other problem concerned the controversially selected Albert Pepperell who had suffered a broken jaw and he was in the same position as was Horne.

The Council had decided that both players would need to face a medical to decide if they were ok to make the journey down to Freemantle. On the 5th April the news broke that Valentine had suffered a broken bone in his spine and would be out for the rest of the season. Had he been selected he would not have been able to go on the tour. I bet one or two selectors breathed a sigh of relief at that news. On the 11th April both Horne and Pepperell faced the doctors and were passed fit. Horne told reporters the finger was healing well but he was having a little trouble handling a ball. Pepperell said his jaw was fine if a bit stiff. Both were advised not to turn out for their clubs and sit tight until they arrived in Australia, which they did.

Back row left to right – Horne-Barrow, Higgins-Widnes, Danby-Salford, Hilton-Wigan, Cunliffe-Wigan, Ryan-Wigan, Pollard-Dewsbury
Third row Naughton-Widnes, Murphy-Wakefield Trinity, Ashcroft-Wigan, Street-Dewsbury, Phillips-Belle Vue Rangers, Triall-Bradford Northern, Ratcliffe-Wigan, Osmond-Swinton
Seated Daniels-Halifax, Ryan-Warrington, Egan-Wigan, Oldroyd-Manager, Ward-Bradford Northern, Spedding-Manager, Gwyther-Belle Vue Rangers, Featherstone-Warrington, Gee-Wigan
Front Pepperell-Workington Town, Bradshaw-Wigan, Ledgard-Leigh, Williams-Leeds

In the wash up of the selection the tour party had seven players in it that were making a second tour down to Australia and New Zealand at that time a record number. They were Ryan the Wigan fullback, along with team mates Ken Gee and Joe Egan. Ward the skipper, Phillips, Horne and Murphy made up the others. Also, it was a measure of the quality of the Wigan team at that time that seven of the players were to go aboard the ship to sail down to the other side of the world. When Hilton, Ratcliffe, Ashcroft and Bradshaw joined their team mates on that day.

On Tuesday the 18th April the tourists all assembled in Leeds to be kitted out for the tour. They left Leeds on the Wednesday by train to London and once they arrived the porters had one hell of a job shifting thirty-five trunks, twenty-six suitcases and dozens of smaller pieces of luggage. In total there was around six tons of clothing and equipment to get to the Himaláya which was to take them down to Australia. The players and the two managers George Oldroyd and Tom Spedding there then taken to the Houses of Parliament where they were welcomed by the then Prime Minister Clement Attlie.

There were three players who had special reasons to be happy at making the tour. Harry Murphy was hoping he had better luck on this tour than had been the case on the 1946 tour. Then in the first game of the tour he had played after twenty minutes he had suffered a broken collar bone and took no further part in the tour. In a similar vein Martin Ryan had played only four games on the previous tour. In the game up in Newcastle he had been kicked in the stomach and it had created a hernia that requires surgery to sort out the problems. The other player was Fred Higgins who was hoping to catch up with an acquaintance down in Sydney who he had served in the Merchant Navy with during the Second World War.

On the 20th April 1950 the tourists went aboard the Himalaya bound for the Antipodes. There were seven Wigan players in the party and there were seven players who were making their second tour down under. Given the fact that the Ashes had been in English hands for thirty years expectations were high that they would remain so. As we shall see the unexpected happened.

CHAPTER TWO
(The Aussie critics suitably impressed with the Englishmen)

The Himalaya followed the same route down to the other side of the world as ships taking previous tourists. They sailed into the Mediterranean and through the Suez Canal and on to Colombo in what is now Sri Lanka. There the players went ashore and were glad to be able to stretch their legs on dry land instead of pounding around the deck of the ship in attempts to keep fit.

In Colombo an impromptu game of touch rugby was organized and twenty of the players took part. There were a number who were still feeling the effects of the injections they were forced to have prior to leaving home. Ken Gee on the other hand was under no illusion with regard to what he intended to do on the trip down. Having seen it all before he had packed his boots in a suitcase labelled "Not needed on Voyage."

As the tourists left Colombo bound for Freemantle they were to do what other tourists before them had done, namely play a low-key game simply to get their land legs. On this trip they were to play a Western Australian side in Perth. Bill Corbett from the Sun Newspaper who was on board the Himalaya with the players kept readers in Sydney up to date with the goings on aboard the ship. On the Friday 12th May just over three weeks after leaving Tilbury the tourists arrived in Freemantle, on the first leg of their journey. They had a training session on the Saturday in preparation for the game against Western Australia.

On the Sunday morning the tourists were picked up by rugby league officials in Perth and taken sightseeing. They eventually arrived at the National Park where preparations for the game would perhaps cause some concern with modern day coaches and players. The reporter for the Sydney Morning Herald wrote:-

"They were driven by cars to National Park where they cooked 50 pounds of steak, chops and sausages barbecue fashion over a roaring fire. To meat rationed Englishmen it was at first startling, then they doffed their blazers and entered fully into the spirit of the proceedings."

Having partaken of a very nice lunch the tourists travelled to the Claremont Showground for the game. The English team for the first match of the tour was:-

Ryan, Daniels, Danby, Ward, Hilton, Williams, Bradshaw, Gee, Osmond, Featherstone, Murphy, Street, Phillips.

Before the kick off the players from both sides were presented to the State Governor Sir James Mitchell. The second row Murphy would have faced the kick-off with more than a little trepidation after his experience on the last tour where he lasted just twenty minutes and was then out for the rest of the tour with a broken collar bone. He need not have worried as the visitors put on a scintillating display of rugby league that simply bamboozled the opposition.

Within the first five minutes of the kick off some razzle-dazzle saw Jack Hilton have the honour of scoring the first try of the tour. Ward tagged on the extras. Williams and Bradshaw simply ran the whole show which ended with a score line of 87-4. Jack Hilton scored seven tries during the afternoon. Daniels on the other wing helped himself to four. The skipper Ward crossed for three tries and kicked twelve goals while Featherstone Osmond and Danby bagged a brace each. Phillips completing the scores with a solo try. It was a good run out against opposition that proved not to be too taxing and augured well for the tougher games to come.

The tourists returned to the Himalaya and sailed on, this time for Melbourne. Corbett writing of the game in the Sun was fulsome in his praise:-

"You can take it from me that the English Rugby League team, which opened its Australian tour here yesterday, will prove itself an 'electric' side in Sydney.

Their main plan is to whirl the ball about- and Lord help the man who is caught in possession.

I have never in my football experience seen such brilliance as Ward's flick-dummy. It twice brought tries yesterday. The bewildering variation of play by

the halves Bradshaw and Williams and the slashing pace, swerve and sidestep of left winger Jack Hilton also were features.

I will make this forecast: This English team will surpass all the post war teams."

It was praise indeed but it was also pointed out that tougher encounters lay ahead. Inevitably the game produced its injuries as Featherstone damaged a knee while Williams suffered a shoulder injury neither were considered to be serious. Sadly, that was not the case for the prop forward Featherstone.

While the ship sailed onto Melbourne Corbett via the ships radio sent a couple of pieces to the Sun which are quite revealing. He wrote a piece about Jack Hilton whose selection had raised more than a little controversy with pundits back in England:-

"He is England's 'flying saucer'. He rotates down the field at a terrific bat with his feet twirling behind him like propeller blades. Hilton has a swerve side step and change of pace but has no idea at what speed he travels, he has never been timed."

Corbett also reveled that some players were still suffering the effects of the vaccinations they had had and that Gordon Ratcliffe was the major concern in that area.

The players arrived in Melbourne and training sessions had been planned for Friday and Saturday to get every player their land legs back. While the players were in

Melbourne on the Saturday a number of them went to watch an Australian Rules Football game. It must be said that they were less than impressed with what was on offer.

The skipper Ernest Ward told Corbett he would rather watch a game of marbles at least that game had some variation. Harry Murphy failed to endear himself to the locals claiming, **"Some of the players should be charged admission. They stand and watch the game as much as the spectators."** The players according to Corbett sat wooden faced throughout the whole match and could not understand why the supporters were cheering or booing events on the field.

Meanwhile Corbett in a second article laid out just how the tourists intended to play their games on the tour:-

"England has abandoned its old principle of tight rugby league football. This season's tourists will keep the ball alive - tactics never seen from an English team in Australia.

Players told me that the methods of the 1946 side that retained the Ashes here were obsolete. There has been a revolution in English strategies, even in the brief period since 1948 when the Australians visited England. They are based on the Lancashire type of football for Lancashire has had to play the fast open game because of its light forwards. But with a blend of big Yorkshire forwards the English pack will take the field to make spectators gasp at their size."

It is an interesting article in so much as it shows a change in emphasis within the English game and perhaps a move toward the more open faster style of play favoured by the Australians. That theme was taken up by the reporter in the Sydney Morning Herald when writing of Martin Ryan the English full back who was revolutionizing the way full backs played the game in England:-

"England's full backs on this tour, Martin Ryan and Jim Ledgard, provide a contrast between the old and new methods of playing the position.

In the Perth match yesterday, Ryan did not kick the ball once but always brought the ball up to the backs. Twice he nearly scored himself.

A Wigan player said later that during the recent English season Ryan would not have kicked the ball a dozen times. He added, possession is the important thing in League football. I believe if the full back keeps the team attacking he is doing the best job.

Ledgard gained his place in the team because of his skill in catching, kicking and touch finding thus saving the forwards. He rarely come up with the ball but is a grand defensive player."

Today such play as was pioneered by Ryan is taken for granted but back in the days of the tour it was a revolutionary new style of play that all full backs would soon adopt both in England and down under.

Dan Naughton hidden and Ken Gee tackle team mate Fred
Higgins during training at Melbourne Cricket Ground
(Photograph printed in Daily Telegraph May 1950)

From Melbourne the players remained aboard the ship
and sailed into Sydney Harbour on Monday the 22nd of
May, they had been at sea a total on just thirty-two days
a far cry from the six weeks or so that pre-war tourists
had been forced to endure. Even as they sailed to the
dock side the first controversy however slight awaited
them. While the players had been up on deck as the ship
entered the harbour to take the obligatory photographs of
the bridge and other sights they had then gone below

deck to have breakfast and finalise packing ready to disembark.

Members of the Australian Board of Control and President Harry Flegg had gone out to the Heads in a launch to escort the ship into dock and were disappointed that the Englishmen had not lined the deck rails to greet them and the public. One of the officials actually got a megaphone and hailed the ship asking **'Is the English team on board?'**

With the tourists now in Sydney the press began to ramp up the publicity machine with stories abounding in the newspapers. Bill Corbett informed his readers of the antics of some of the players. He told of Dickie Williams the stand-off being so conscious of his big front teeth that he had taken to wearing a mouth guard similar to those used by boxers to protect them. Big Ken Gee on his second tour had been a revelation back home with his goal kicking. In a very successful season for his Wigan club he had kicked one hundred and thirty-three goals. He puts his success down to his mentor the great Jim Sullivan.

The vice-captain Joe Egan was so keen to make a return tour to Australia that he gave up his job as a brass founder. He was convinced that the brass dust was affecting his breathing so he became a full-time footballer living off the money he earned from the game. All the players when they were told that a player-coach in Australia could earn £20 per week were astounded claiming that £12 was considered to be good money back in England. There were similar articles in other newspapers.

This was the sort of publicity which greeted the players when they disembarked in Sydney. They were then transported to the Coogee Bay Hotel which was to be their headquarters for the tour. They were also given permission by Randwick Council to use the Coogee Oval as their training base. What surprised the players about this was that the Oval was the home of Randwick Rugby Union Club. In Australia the two codes seemed to be quite happy to co-exist side by side unlike back home where the war had been stepped up between the two codes since the end of the Second World War. They would not find the same camaraderie when they got down to New Zealand.

On that evening the players were entertained at the New South Wales Rugby League club and when they arrived they were surprised to see great platters filled with chicken and turkey drum sticks. The meat starved players needed no second invitation to demolish what was placed in front of them. The managers had other matters to attend to however. The first thing was to set up a meeting with the Australian Board to iron out different interpretations of the rules. The tourists intended to follow the lead of the 1946 tourists who for the first time had abandoned the 'we invented the rules so we should all play to them' attitude in favour of playing to the local rules. That being the case they needed to get the players used to the differing approach to the scrum and play the ball rules amongst others.

There was also one more area of contention that being the rule concerning a forward pass. In England the rule was simple, any and all forward passes resulted in the referee ordering a scrum. That was not the case in Australia where referees would order a scrum only if the pass was deemed not to be deliberate. If the referee decided a pass was deliberately forward then a penalty would be awarded for the player receiving the ball being off side. Both Oldroyd and Spedding were wanting a clear interpretation just how or what constituted a deliberate forward pass. To that end it was decided that a top referee would visit the players and explain the local interpretation. Sadly, this was a problem that simply would not go away and referees frustrated the tourists with their rulings all through the tour.

There was also a problem with the ball used in the Australian game which was a little smaller than that used in England. The ball used in France was smaller and lighter still and about the same size as that used up in Queensland while that used in New Zealand was longer and narrower than those in use in Sydney. All were agreed that there needed to be some standard of uniformity with regard to the ball.

With all these problems discussed if not sorted out, serious training being undertaken by the players and the itinerary firmed up. All that remained was the official reception by the Lord Mayor of Sydney. That completed the tour could now begin in earnest.

CHAPTER THREE

**(Trouble with referees, injuries, a cancelled game but tourists
are unbeaten in NSW)**

The second game of the tour was to be played down in the nation's capital Canberra against Monaro. The Australian Board had arranged for the players to be flown down to Canberra and to return to Sydney the same day again by air. The two managers set about selecting a team bearing in mind that the first priority was to win the game but equally important was to ensure every player got a game under their belt as soon as possible. That being the case the players who had face Western Australia tended not to figure in selection When training finished on the Tuesday and the managers, captain and vice-captain sat down to select the side Ken Gee had other matters to attend to on his mind. He met up with the Aussie winger Johnny Graves at training and afterwards bought him a schooner or two of the amber nectar. He did so to fulfil a promise he had made to Graves at Odsal Stadium back home when the third Test had been postponed. Gee had promised to buy the beer if he were to get selected for the tour.

On the Wednesday the team selected to meet Monaro flew down to Canberra for the game. The match was played at the Manuka Oval and the players had a full day. All were only too aware that in truth the tour really started with the game that afternoon. On arrival in Canberra the tourists set about preparing for the first game in New South Wales. Prior to the game a number of people accompanying the tourists met up with the players. One of them was Tom Fallowfield the father of the present Secretary of the Rugby League Bill Fallowfield. Tom Fallowfield a half back had actually played against the original Kangaroos brought over by James Giltinan in 1908-09 at Barrow. Others in the party included the Leigh Chairman James Hilton, Walter Crockford from the Hull club a former Chairman of the Rugby League. The pair were part of the selection committee for the present tour.

The thirteen that were to meet Monaro in what was really the first important game of the tour were:-

Ledgard, Pollard, Cunliffe, Ashcroft, Ratcliffe, Horne, Pepperell, Naughton, Egan, Gwyther, Higgins, Ryan, Traill.

Ken Traill was particularly pleased to be in the team as he had been suffering with a painful arm following the adverse reaction to vaccinations received back in England. The area of the injection had become infected and had troubled him all the way down to Australia. He was desperate to get a game under his belt as competition for Test places was expected to be fierce. The doctor was happy to allow him to play with a pad over the affected part of the upper arm.

When the game kicked off the was a steady drizzle that had been going on for a couple of hours and the ball was greasy and heavy as a result. The English were expected to benefit from the conditions but their handling was not up to the standard expected from an international outfit. The players should have expected that all would not go well for just before the game the referee originally schedule to take charge by the name of Lee was taken ill. A young local referee Alan Nicholls took the whistle and blew it with monotonous regularity. He constantly penalized Albert Pepperell for illegal feeding at the scrum and the constant scrummaging seemed to affect Joe Egan who instead of dominating the scrum could only come up with a 50% share.

The Monaro team had set their stall out to defend and defend they did, constantly thwarting the visitors. The other thing that annoyed the players was that they had agreed to the Australian ruling that for a deliberate forward pass a penalty would be given rather than a scrum as it was back home. On a number of occasions, the pass was only inches forward and in no way deliberate but the referee gave a penalty on each and every occasion. There was however a stranger problem to be overcome. As half time was approaching supporters began waiting for the whistle to end the first half. They waited and they waited as did the authorities but no whistle came. As the half went on a frantic search began for the official time keeper but it was all in vain. No one seemed to know just who the time keeper was or if one had actually been appointed. Finally, after forty-eight minutes a frantic official took the initiative, rang the bell and the referee blew to end the first half with the score at 16-4 to the tourists.

The game itself began in the drizzle and from the first scrum England were penalized and the Monaro player James kicked for goal. The kick fell short and Ledgard collected the ball and proceeded to run it out, his pass to Cunliffe was ruled forward and a penalty awarded again to the home side. The resulting penalty goal gave them the lead 2-0. That seemed to spur the visitors on and a few minutes later Ratcliffe crossed for a converted try to take the lead 2-5. From yet another penalty the home side closed the gap to 4-5.

The visitors were looking non-plussed at the referee's interpretation of the rules and were getting frustrated particularly as it seemed each and every forward pass resulted in a penalty for off side. It was skipper Egan that calmed the players down when he intercepted a pass and set off down field. He passed to Traill who went over unopposed for another converted try. As the long first half came to a conclusion, Ashcroft and Pollard had scored tries but Ledgard had been unable to convert so as the players left the field the score line read 4-16. In the second half the tourists took control and eventually ran out winners 10-37. Traill and Pollard scored a double while Ashcroft, Ryan, Egan, Ratcliffe and Higgins got a try each. Jim Ledgard kicked five goals and by all accounts appeared to have played particularly well.

There was one interesting incident that came out of the game and it was connected with the scorer of Monaro's only try Bill McKell. McKell was the son of the Governor-General of New South Wales at the time. It was though an unconvincing performance, patchy at times with handling errors aplenty. It was however, a win and any win particularly so soon into the tour was welcomed by the players. The press had mixed views on the performance some critical others of the opinion that players were still trying to get their land legs.

With the game over the players were entertained at a cocktail party by Mr. E. K. Williams The High Commissioner for the United Kingdom in Parliament House. It was then on to a dinner hosted by the Leagues Group. The Minister for the Navy and the Minister for Supply were the guests of honour and when the manager Tom Spedding stood up to respond to a speech, he was interrupted mid-speech by the entrance of the Australian Prime Minister Robert Menzies. Menzies delighted the players by giving an impromptu 'whimsical' speech in which he said he had just come from 'a scrum'-a party meeting. The following day the players flew back to Sydney to prepare for the game on the Saturday against Newcastle. Both the press and the players were of the opinion that this game would be the first real test for the tourists.

Loose forward Harry Street tackles Harry Murphy
(Photograph printed from Daily Telegraph May 1950)

On the last two tours in 1936 and ten years later the Newcastle side had got the better of the Englishmen and hopes were high for a hat-trick victory. The two managers were not about to let that happen and took the decision to select a strong side. Traill who had damaged his chest down in Canberra and Featherstone who had not fully recovered from the twisted knee in Perth were not considered. In the 1946 game Martin Ryan had been injured and took no further part in the rest of the tour while Phillips had received his marching orders that afternoon. The managers appeared to have taken the view discretion was the better part of valour and excluded the pair from the team.

In an interview with the press Ward the English skipper put down the idea that Newcastle had a 'hoodoo' over the English as they had beaten them in the past two tours. He also ridiculed the suggestion that the team selected to play up in Newcastle was the 'Test team'. As we shall see it was a claim that simply would not go away as the tour progressed with reporters claiming that two teams existed if only in the minds of the two managers. It was the reporter on the Daily Telegraph that first publicized this growing division within the party. George Crawford when writing of hooker Joe Egan being selected for the game against Newcastle said:-

"Selection of experienced hooker over Frank Osmond for the second match this week is significant. Egan won a place in the touring team only on a casting vote but selectors are apparently already grooming him for the Tests."

Perhaps rather than selectors it would be more apt to use the term managers. As the tour progressed it was a claim that would be made with regard to quite a number of other players who seemed only to figure in the lesser games.

Ward did admit that the players were expecting a hard game and said they would discuss tactics once they were in the dressing room and had seen the state of the pitch. When the team took to the field they did so in front of a record crowd estimated to be around 26,000. The bugbear for the English managers was that at such games all ground members were allowed in free as were players so while contributing to the gate they added nothing to the receipts! Hundreds of supporters had climbed up onto the roof of the grandstand and a number of sheds inside the ground to get a better view. At one time during the game when the home side scored and looked like they could pull the game out of the fire the crowd stormed the touch line. They were cheering on their heroes and felt they could defeat the visitors for a third consecutive time. As the game was ending the noise was so loud that the referee could not hear the bell being rung by the time keeper to end the game. It took over a minute to attract the attention of the referee who then blew to end the game.

Once again, the game was won 21-10 but it was again not a good performance and the press did not wrap it up either. For the majority of the game the English faced just twelve men. After five minutes the home wingman Bunt was tackled on the touch line and a team mate stood on his hand. The result was a gash requiring five stitched and he took no further part in the game. The Newcastle skipper brought a forward out to play on the wing and it has to be said that the five home forwards more than held their own against the English six. It was left to the silky skills of the backs to pull the game out of the fire. The undoubted star was Ashcroft who was in everything that was good. He put his Wigan team mate and wing partner Jack Hilton in for three tries. Joe Egan got in the act with a try as did Ashcroft himself. Ernest Ward slotted over three goals.

As the half time whistle blew the score line was 13-0 to the tourists and with just over ten minutes remaining in the game they were leading 21-0. The Newcastle side then staged a revival and scored two converted tries to take the score to 21-10. The question was, did the English simply take their foot off the gas with the game wrapped up or was their fitness letting them down? The press was of the latter opinion The Local reporter in Newcastle 'Galago' best summed up the game:-

"The British Rugby League team which defeated Newcastle 21-10, left an impression of disappointing forwards, of a smoothly working set of backs, with great individual brilliance, and of a team that which needs solid training before it faces the big games."

It was criticism the managers were aware of for they had taken the decision to reduce the number of social gatherings the players were to attend as the training racked up in preparation for the fast approaching first Test. The game also with that inevitability that pervades the game produced its injuries. Pollard turned an ankle which at first was thought not to be serious but he did not finish the game. Ward also went down with severe cramp which was not something that normally affected him. Pollard was to be assessed once he returned to Sydney.

Cartoon by Ron Madden after the Newcastle Game
(Printed in the Newcastle Herald May 1950)

When the team returned to Sydney there were two little snippets that Bill Corbett revealed to his readers. In conversation with Fred Higgins the player revealed that his tour selection had been predicted by Fred De Belin. The two had opposed each other when the Kangaroos played Lancashire. After the game De Belin said to Higgins 'See you in Australia in 1950". Not me mate came the response from Higgins. He had made frequent visits to Australia while serving in the Merchant Navy in World War Two.

The other snippet concerned the Prop Elwyn Gwyther whose surname or rather its pronunciation was a cause of concern for folks in Sydney. As Corbett pointed out, in his native Wales it was pronounced GWI THER, in England it was pronounced GWY THER. When Corbett asked him what he liked to be called his reply was 'I don't mind but don't call me before seven in the morning.'

With the squad together in Coogee the feeling was that the tour had gone as well as could be hoped for three games played three games won. It was true the team had not really gelled yet but it was early days and play would get better. Now there was a game down in Cootamundra against Riverina to prepare for. It was a measure of just how seriously country sides were taking games against the touring party as they had hired a coach to prepare them for the encounter. It was not just any coach either it was Len Smith the former International coach and player who had sensationally not been selected for the tour to England in 1948 in the most controversial of circumstances.

Smith had captained the Australian team in two Tests against New Zealand just prior to the 1948 tour party being selected. Not only was he the captain but had been designated the coach as well. When the tour party had been revealed he was not in the team. It seems in the space of a couple of weeks he had gone from captain/coach to not being good enough to win a place on the tour. Rumours and inuendo flew about, the strongest being that he had not been selected simply because he was a Roman Catholic while the majority of the selectors were Freemasons. He was still very well respected in the game hence his selection for the coaching position.

For the game the managers appointed The Welsh forward Doug Phillips to lead the side. It was the first time he had been given that honour. What the lead up revealed was just how the Australians were preparing for each and every game against the tourists. Vic Hey the former Leeds and Australian stand-off had been appointed the coach of the national side while the tourists were preparing to leave for Australia. Smith who was writing a column in the Sun newspaper had watched the tourists play a great deal and was beginning to see which players were doing well and those that were not. His insights were to be valuable to the Riverina side that afternoon.

There was a little light relief for the touring party on that Monday evening as they went to watch Western Suburbs play Glebe in an ice hockey game. Ernest Ward did the honours by walking onto the ice to start the proceedings much to the amusement of his team mates. The following day it was revealed that after examination Pollard's ankle was worse than first thought and he was being ruled out of the first Test just a couple of weeks away. Pollard like all players was far more optimistic claiming he was feeling better. The two managers created their own little piece of history on that Tuesday when given the names of three referees from which to select the man to referee the first Test. They decided that George Bishop was their preferred choice to referee the up coming Test. By doing so they made Bishop the very first Australian Test player to referee a Test Match. Bishop had played at hooker in 1933 in a Test match. Webby Neill had on earlier tours refereed Test games and while a Kangaroo having toured England in 1911-12 he had never played in a Test match. The newspapers also revealed that Vic Hey the national coach had approached his club Parramatta for leave in order to travel down to Cootamundra to watch the tourists play first hand.

The game also saw Martin Ryan the Wigan full back play his first game on the tour. Great play was made of the fact that he had a 'dicky' shoulder and would be wearing protection. He had broken a collar bone earlier in the season back home but had recovered sufficiently to gain a place on the tour. However, it was noted in training that he tended to favour the affected shoulder and avoided making any vigorous tackles. It was also pointed out that while he had been injured Jack Cunliffe had stood in at full back and played very well.

As the players took to the field at Fisher Park, they did so in front of around 8,000 supporters who cheered madly as the home side resplendent in their gold and maroon jerseys took to the field. When the game began it quickly became apparent just what Len Smith wanted his team to do. The three quarters stood up as close to the advantage line as was possible and were quick to move up and tackle the English backs. The other thing that was apparent was that the referee was seemingly penalizing the visitors for offences at the scrum and play the ball with monotonous regularity. The players were increasingly getting more confused by his decisions.

The English led by Pepperell and Horne began however to take control and with deft dummy runs and scissor movement baffled the opposition and as half time approached, they were leading 13-4 and seemingly in total control. Just before half time Horne threw out a wild pass which was intercepted and to the delight of the home crowd the try and goal took the half-time score to just 13-9 The only worry was that Danby took a knock to the shoulder and was struggling in the game. In the second half Pollard who had surprised every one by being declared fit made the best run of the game but while the game was won 23-13 it had not been a great performance yet again.

Len Smith gained a great deal of praise for the game plan he came up with to nullify the visitors. He was pleased and felt that stronger teams would have capitalized more on the mistakes the tourists made during the match. The Riverina authorities made a huge offer to Smith to move to Cootamundra and coach the schools and the clubs in the area following the game. Smith declined the offer but he showed quite clearly just what type of plan was needed to beat the Englishmen.

As was ever the case the game took its toll on the visitors with the winger Ratcliffe damaging a thumb. The centre Danby injured a shoulder while the scrum half Pepperell received a cut over his right eye as did Ryan the full back. They joined Featherstone and Traill on the injured list and the tour had only really got started. Sadly, the wingmen in particular were to suffer greatly as the tour progressed.

Following the game, the team to meet NSW at the Cricket Ground on the Saturday was named and Crawford once again in the Daily Telegraph referred to it as 'The Test Team'. He commented that Tom Spedding was keen to get the full back Ryan into form in preparation for the Test. Ryan had not had the best of games against Riverina often mis-judging the ball when kicked to him or being caught in possession. Once again though we see how the players were being 'segregated' by the managers into Test and mid-week teams.

The great Eddie Waring writing also in the Daily Telegraph was less than happy with the performance of the Englishmen. In particular he felt that Ryan had played poorly and put it down to a lack of confidence. He was though very impressed with the coach Len Smith as he felt the Riverina side had 'out marshalled' the tourists and had the best idea of how to play tactical football from any country side he had ever seen. He along with others expressed the opinion that the referee had been a little too fond of the whistle during the game and that had not helped the flow of play.

One little mystery was cleared up in the Sun on the 31st May, namely just why every one rushed to sit next to Frank Osmond the English hooker at meal times. It would appear that he was not a meat lover much preferring an apple and bread and butter! As he told a reporter:-

"If meat is served I may eat a little as a matter of course. All the way from home the boys have been talking about the food to be had in Australia with emphasis on the steaks. They can have my share of the steaks. My idea of a satisfying meal is to munch on an apple and eat bread and butter with it."

The reporter not without a sense of humour obviously, reported **'Osmond at least should be safe from one accusation, he is never likely to be charged with ear-biting in the scrum.'** It was obvious his team mates did not share his philosophy as it was revealed at the recent reception held by the Board of Control for the touring party some three hundred weight of food was disposed of meat and all!

A good many of the players who played down in Cootamundra were disappointed with their performances as well as that of the team as a whole. The only good thing was as they say 'any win is a good win' and they were still undefeated. The ante was without doubt about to be upped for on the Saturday they were to face New South Wales in what was without a shadow of a doubt the hardest game of the tour to date. It was also one that was crucial to the further success of the tour. A win would see the tour financially secure, defeat could very well jeopardize that.

On the Friday at practice the two packs of forwards carried out a great deal of scrummaging practice. They and the managers knew full well that if they did not get it right on the Saturday they could well get penalized out of the game. The other area that was worked on was the play the ball. In England the players were allowed to place the ball on the ground behind their foot in Australia it had to be placed on the ground in front of the foot. Easy to explain difficult to carry out in the heat of a game.

Bill Corbett who watched the practice and later spoke with Vic Hey who was to coach New South Wales along with the national side. As he told Hey the side that will face the state side will be a different one to that played down in Cootamundra. Hey's reply was that the tactics employed would be the same. In assessing the game Corbett felt that the odds favoured the tourists. The one area he felt the English were superior was in the fact that they played a left and right centre pair whereas the Australians still persevered with an inside and outside centre. In his opinion the English centres had a better understanding with their respective wingmen. The tourists had named seven forwards for the game simply because Doug Phillips had suffered an arm injury against the Riverina and if fit he would play if not then his replacement was already in the team.

The other area of play that the tourists needed to work on was that in the ruck. In the games played so far, they had played a very loose game with on many occasions, forwards throwing out long lobbed passes from the ruck to the backs. This would leave them open to possible interceptions when they faced the faster stronger team. It was the prop Gwyther who summed up the new approach to be adopted when he told the reporters:-

"We have had a good runaround to get into form. On Saturday we will be getting down to the more serious business of our tour. You will not see anything loose about our play in the big matches."

It would appear that the players fully intended to tighten up all areas of their game as the serious part of the tour was upon them.

As kick-off approached at the Sydney Cricket Ground all roads were jam packed with folks making their way to the game. The long lines at every turn stile would have pleased the authorities as a bumper receipt was guaranteed. By the time the game kicked off there was a crowd of 70.419 packed into the ground who had paid some £8,911 for the privilege of watching the encounter. It was a record crowd even for Sydney that cheered the two teams onto the pitch. The English team that afternoon was:-

Ryan, Pollard, Ward, Ashcroft, Hilton, Williams, Bradshaw, Gee, Egan, Gwyther, Ryan, Higgins and Street.

Phillips was not considered to have recovered sufficiently from the arm injury.

Once the game began it was quickly obvious to all on the ground just what the New South Wales tactics were to be. The backs stood up in a line as close the advantage line as possible and once the tourist backs got the ball they 'spotted' them. The tactics worked for the silky skills of the English backs were not seen in the first forty minutes. Early in the half the state centre Johnny Hawke damaged a knee and he was unable to continue.

When the home side gained possession the two half backs simply put short grubber kicks in behind the English three quarter line forcing then to turn round. Bradshaw was also earning the wrath of the referee George Bishop for the way he was feeding the scrums. The first half turned out to be a half of penalties. Most of the attacking football on display came from the visitors the home side were being kept in the game by the penalties. From five such penalties Pidding slotted over three and Ward was successful with just one. When the teams took the half-time break, the score was 6-2 in favour of the home side.

The half-time break saw supporters entertained by a big fight that took place on the hill while in another part of the ground supporters were jumping around as someone let off fire crackers. In the tourists dressing room the doctor was looking at the winger Pollard who yet again had been injured late in the first half. It was discovered that he had dislocated his collar bone and his tour effectively could be over. Harry Street was pulled from the scrum and replaced Pollard on the wing. When the two teams went out for the second stanza they were both down to twelve men as Hawke was a limping passenger out there just he make a nuisance of himself.

Not long into the half Street was pulled out by the referee and cautioned, from the resulting penalty Pidding increased the lead to 8-2. Things were looking a little bleak for the visitors and something needed to be done. A number of fights broke out as frustration on both sides grew. After one such altercation Hawke finally limped from the field never to return. From a penalty some forty yards out Ken Gee attempted to kick the goal only to see the ball hit an upright and bounce out. Ward was injured after a heavy tackle and needed attention but up to this point in the game the football was not of a high standard. There were pieces of brilliance from Williams and Bradshaw but these were few and far between. Ward converted a short-range penalty to take the score to 8-4.

At last the tourists managed to trouble the scoreboard when Ryan at full back collected yet another kick through. He ran the ball back and passed the ball to Ashcroft who feigned to go left and then cut inside Churchill to score the first try of the game by the posts. With Ward adding the extras the visitors had the lead for the first time all be it a slender one at 8-9. The Englishmen now began to keep the ball in the scrummages drawing in defenders. Then Bob Ryan the second row threw out a long pass to Ward who in one movement collected and passed the ball on to Ashcroft. Ashcroft equally as speedily fed Hilton his wingman who did the rest, crossing in the corner for an unconverted try and a score line of 8-12.

The visitors were now in the ascendency and when Ward took another long pass that cut out two Englishmen he used Street as a foil and dummied to cross for his sides third try. He also added the extras and the lead had stretched out to 8-17. With the game coming to a close an English try begun once again by Ashcroft after he intercepted a pass was scored. He slipped through the defense and was supported by Hilton who had come all the way across from his left wing position. Ashcroft coolly drew the full back before releasing Hilton for his second try. In the last ten minutes of the game the Englishmen had crossed for three tries and taken the game away from the home side. A try by the home side wingman Troy on the full-time bell was a consolation effort that took the score to 11-20. Pidding stepped up to convert the final try. As the ball soared over the cross bar all the Englishmen leapt high in an attempt to get the ball to keep as a souvenir. The touch judge Jack Kelly beat them all, after signaled a goal he grabbed the ball and stuffed it up his jersey. For the visitors the game had been won 13-20 and they remained undefeated.

While it would be true to say that the whole team had played well in parts all the reporters were of one opinion. In their eyes two players had stood out above the rest in a great team performance. Bob Ryan in the second row must have covered every blade of grass and often broke clear in the ruck making twenty or thirty yards before releasing his backs. The other player was Bradshaw who was to say the least dynamic. He would often start a move from the ruck and race away behind his fast-moving backs to be on hand to take the ball and start yet another attack. As one reporter wrote 'he never seemed to be more than two or three yards from where ever the ball was.' Mind you he did get a cut to the eyelid that required stitching for his troubles!

The whole tour party were delighted with the hard fought win and it was difficult to criticize the players but there were problems both on and off the field. On the field it had taken around twenty-six minutes of the second half before the English had breached the New South Wales line. While it was true, they then went on to score three more in the closing stages the tactics devised by coach Vic Hey had worked for most of the game as had those of Smith down in the Riverina. The problems off the field were simple enough there was a shortage of a left wingmen in the party. Daniels had damaged an ankle which ruled him out of the up coming Test. Pollard would also be out for a minimum of five weeks with a dislocated collar bone.

Ratcliffe could play on the left as he had often done for Wigan back home but the managers decided that in the mid-week game against Western Division at Forbes they would see how Tom Danby went in the left wing berth.

Danby was no stranger to the position as it was on the wing that he had earned an England rugby union cap. Given that Ratcliffe was selected on the right wing at Forbes it would seen Danby was being looked on as the Test winger come the first Test. The managers had a bit of a dilemma, it was difficult to criticize the players after all they were to date undefeated. The problem was that the tactics teams were employing against them were in the main working they were stifling the three quarters for large parts of games.

Bill Corbett in the Sun was still extoling the virtues of the visitors in his daily column. He felt that in the up coming Test to be played on the Monday the players would be fitter and faster than when they beat New South Wales. Watching the tourists work out in training at the Cricket Ground he felt they were the finest he had seen in a touring side. There was more good news when it was revealed that Daniels ankle was improving faster than expected and given the extra two days with the Test on the Monday his chances of playing had greatly improved. It was however expected that the second Test was a more realistic prospect. On the down side Tommy Bradshaw had two stiches inserted into a cut over his eye from the game on the weekend. By Tuesday the eye had swollen and he could not see out of it but was expected to be fine for the Test.

If the managers were hoping that they would be able to assess just how well young Danby went they were to be sadly disappointed. The plan had been to take only the players needed for the game against Western District and for the remainder to stay in Sydney and continue preparations for the Test match. Sadly, as is always the case if the unexpected can disrupt it will disrupt. The arrangements made by the Australian Board and the two managers was to fly the players out west and fly them back. A Dakota aircraft was chartered from Mascot and took off late due to the bad weather. The problem was that the further west it flew the further the weather deteriorated. By the time they approached Parkes Airport visibility was so poor the pilot made the decision it was too dangerous to land and turned the aircraft round and attempted to find a suitable landing place.

For the players on the Butler Airways Dakota it would have been a very unnerving situation that they found themselves in. As they flew over Parkes attempting to locate the airstrip the air traffic controllers in Sydney instructed the pilot to divert to Mangelore in Victoria. The pilot could not locate the airstrip there also and was then diverted to Dubbo. On arriving at Dubbo, they found that airport closed to traffic due to the weather. The pilot was then informed that the airport at Wagga Wagga was open so flew there. He landed the aircraft and re-fueled before taking off once more heading once again for Parkes. On arrival once again, the weather was so bad the airstrip could not be seen. The attempt to land was abandoned and the plane and the players returned to Sydney. It is difficult to assess the feelings of the players many of whom would never have experienced such a flight. In truth not that many of them would have been on an airplane before. We know a few were ill with air sickness while others were a little wary about flying in such conditions.

On arriving in Sydney, the manager Tom Spedding telephoned officials in Forbes and promised to do every thing possible to re-arrange the fixture. As could be expected the officials at Forbes were less than happy at the decision and made their feelings known to the Australian Board. They felt that with country games the team should be in town the day before the game. In typical Aussie fashion though they continued with the after- match banquet and speeches. Sadly, as we now know it proved impossible to rearrange the fixture with Western Suburbs.

Following the abortive mission to Forbes the two managers announced the team that would take to the field in the first Test on the Monday to the waiting press. Discretion would appear to have been the better part of valour in the minds of the managers and they opted for Ratcliffe on the left wing. After all they had not had a chance to assess how Danby would fare on the wing the game at Forbes being aborted. On the Friday the players trained on the Coogee Oval and eyed with some pleasure the sky.

There had been a great deal of rain in Sydney and that had made the Cricket Ground very wet and heavy conditions that the tourists were used to and the host not.

At one point the ground had resembles a lake but it did drain well. The authorities however conscious of the Test on the Monday were making efforts to get the main league game on Saturday transferred from the Cricket Ground to the Sports Ground. Balmain and South Sydney were due to meet and the fear was that they would cut up the ground, sadly the Trustees at the Cricket Ground refused to transfer the match so it was to go ahead on the Saturday.

As the players had a rare Saturday off, they were allowed a little relaxation and on that Friday attended a lunch at Anthony Hordens. In the evening the were guests of honour at a banquet held at Tattersall's City Club in Sydney. Following the Test match on the Tuesday they were to be guests of the Governor-General Mr McKell at Admiralty House. On that Tuesday like other tour parties had done before them they were to stop off at Martin Place and lay a wreath at the Cenotaph. As this was going on the rain was still falling.

As the Test got closer anyone who was anyone was speculating as to the out come of the game. What tactics would the tourists adopt, what would the home side do to counter act the silky smooth three quarters and the running of full back Martin Ryan. On the eve of the game the Sunday Sun had a full page spread in which Duncan Thompson, Len Smith and Harry Sunderland had their say. All three were of the opinion that the game would be closer than many expected. The newspaper even had pictures in sequence of some of the moves the visitors had been practicing out at Coogee and had been seen in previous games they had played. Going into the game spirits were high in the tourist camp after all they were unbeaten so far and this leading into the first Test. Not only that but God must really be an Englishman for he had even orchestrated the weather to suit them.

It was Duncan Thompson who gave the best insight into just what the English men would do in the game:-

"By various moves they will try to work our defence one way, then attack in another.
Use the long pass to cut out a man.
Bring the full back into the attack to make an extra man.
Carry the ball in the hands not in the arms, to give a quick transfer.
Use close passing amongst the forwards to keep the ball moving and not let it go to ground any more than possible.
Back up intensely in attack and defence."

It was a pretty good assessment of the English style of play at that time. It seems the days of scrums and rucks were being phased out in the English game. It was for that very reason than some of the players were expressing the view that the weather and heavy ground would actually work against them and their style of play.

Monday morning dawned to grey skies and a steady trickle of rain. That did not deter hundreds of hardy supporters some who had been waiting for the turn styles to open at seven in the morning. The continual rain was causing concern for the officials who decided that an inspection of the ground was required. What they saw caused them to tell the press that conditions were "shocking". However, the decision was made to let the game go ahead, in truth there was little else they could do the schedule for the tour was so tight that to fit in a Test mid-week would be a financial disaster in the making. Given the ground conditions one decision the authorities made would seem to beggar belief. They allowed the two warm up games scheduled to go ahead and add to the churning up of the sodden pitch. One thing was certain the downpours during the morning deterred many fans from attending the game. There were just 47,215 hardy souls in the ground to greet the two teams:

England

Ryan, Ratcliffe, Ward, Ashcroft, Hilton, Williams, Bradshaw, Gwyther, Egan, Gee, Higgins, Ryan, Street.

Australia

Churchill, McRichie, Middleton, Pidding, Troy, Stanmore, Holman, Hall, Schubert, Holland, de Bellin, Thompson, Cowie.

When the game kicked off the English team had seven players from the Wigan club and that was eight if you consider that Ryan the second row had learned his rugby in Wigan before signing for Warrington.

It quickly became obvious that open football was not going to be very possible but no one told the players. Very quickly the pitch became a sea of black soup. The players were covered in black mud and it was impossible to distinguish friend from foe. Official began placing buckets filled with water along the touchline to enable players to wash the mud from their eyes. The game began with the Australians attacking and the tourists counter attacking. Penalties were frequent and in the first ten minutes Pidding took a shot at goal. Scraping away the mud he placed the ball and let fly. To the disappointment of the crowd the ball swerved away at the last second to be waved away by the touch judges. He was to suffer a similar fate a couple of minutes later when from in front of the posts and only thirty-five yards out he saw the ball hit the cross bar and bounce back infield.

The visitors were on the wrong side of an increasing penalty count that was constantly putting them on the back foot. It was they who were to score first in the game and a beauty it was to. From a ruck on the Australian twenty-five yard line England won quick clean ball. The ball was sped out to Ashcroft who drew the defence and raced down the left wing. He held the ball for what seemed like an age until Hilton was in the right position. Ashcroft's pass sent Hilton racing for the corner. He pulled out of Holman's covering tackle to score in the corner. Not unexpectedly Ward could not convert the try but the visitors were in the lead 3-0.

The game became fierce with no quarter asked from both sets of forwards. Once again England were penalized and the skipper Ward approached the referee to ask just what the penalty was for. Pidding simply got on with the job of lining up the ball and this time he put it through the posts to close the score to 3-2. Following the penalty play from both sides became much rougher and fists and boots flew. Thirty minutes into the game the Australians got yet another penalty and Pidding stepped up once again and slotted over a magnificent kick in the conditions. The hosts had the lead at 4-3 for the first time in the game.

The goal spurred on the Australian players to greater efforts in an attempt to secure a further score. As the battle raged the two opposing stand-off halfs Stanmore and Williams were dictating play with short kicks in behind the opposition and in Williams case by cleverly turning the ball back inside to his forwards for them to run onto. With the half running out and Australian on the attack the whole game was stood on its head. The Australians were battering the tourists try line and it seemed inevitable that they would score.

Hall the Australian prop threw out a wild pass which Ashcroft intercepted and set off down field to the opposite try line. As he approached the half way line and got into enemy territory Stanmore pulled off a cover tackle and seemed to have saved the situation. Hilton however had reacted to the interception and come off his own wing to move across to the other side of the field to support Ashcroft. As Ashcroft was falling to the ground he threw out a pass to Hilton. The "English Flying Saucer" caught the ball with ease and raced to the try line. Holman made a desperate attempt at a cover tackle but suffered the same fate as he had when Hilton had scored his first try. Ward once more failed with the conversion but as the teams went in for the half time break England led the game 6-4.

The second half saw both sides take to the field with clean shirts and shorts with the exception of the massive prop Ken Gee who only changed his shirt. It made little difference as within minutes the players were once again indistinguishable from each other. Both sides had chances to score but with time running out it was the hosts who had the better of the exchanges. In an attacking movement early in the half the Aussie prop Jack Holland looked to have slid across the line to score a vital try as he and Ashcroft went to ground the ball. Ratcliffe covering kicked the loose ball over the try line and claimed the ball had been dislodge in the collision with Ashcroft. Ratcliffe then grounded the ball over his own try line. The referee Bishop agreed with the wingman and awarded no try and a drop out from under the post by the tourists.

From yet one more penalty again thirty-five yards out Pidding saw his attempt agonizingly hit the post and bounce back into the field of play. With the game coming to a close England were penalized inside their own twenty-five yard area for a play the ball infringement. Pidding stepped up and the whole ground held its breath. To the delight of the visitors the ball once again sailed wide. When the bell sounded and the referee blew for the end of the game the tourists were still unbeaten.

There is no doubt that the win was a great one given the conditions certainly the tourists were on the wrong end of a 19 to 2 penalty count through out the game which stifled their attack even in the mud. There was another factor that contributed to the win that was Joe Egan winning the scrums thirty-nine to twenty-seven. That domination ensured the visitors were able to play the game tight during the second period. It was probably the best start to a tour that any visiting party had since the tours began.

Following the game, the recriminations began. Jack Holland was adamant that he had scored a vital try in the sixth minute of the second half claiming he had dived on the ball and slide across the try line with ball in hand. The English were adamant that a great many of the penalties they had conceded were unwarranted. It was a difficulty they had not expected and their argument was that while a good number of the penalties could have been justified it seemed the referee was not so strict on the home side. They were annoyed that the Australians were allowed to stand up close and also barge at the play the ball area.

The skipper Ward told reporters that it was the most treacherous pitch he had ever played on:-

"I have had games in England which have exhausted me more, through a combination of wet and extreme cold. But for sheer difficulty in maintaining foothold and holding on to passes, today's ordeal was unsurpassed in my experience."

The reporter in the Sydney Morning Herald reckoned the best two players on the pitch were the oldest and youngest English forwards, Ken Gee and Harry Street. He wrote, **'Sixteen stone Gee showed wonderful stamina and bursts of speed and England kept the ball tight in the second half. Twenty-two year old Street kept his feet amazingly well in the mud and showed skill as well as resolution in his co-operation with Bradshaw at the base of the scrum. Street's selection for the tour was severely criticized in England. But he is turning out to be one of the outstanding successes.'**

The Australian pundits to their credit were all of the opinion that the best team won. Tom Gorman wrote **'England were the better side. They played to their well-known pattern for a wet day'**. Colin Maxwell the 1948 tour skipper said, **'Australia were unlucky, but England always seemed to have that extra bit, and can turn defense into attack.'** The great Dave Brown was of the opinion, **'England were more adaptable, Gwyther and Street were outstanding.'**

The former Kangaroo Ray Stehr felt that. **'We were just not good enough.'** Walter Poppelwell who had managed the last tour by the Englishman was ecstatic and said, **'England's forwards were the key to the game, especially the way they brought the ball out of danger. Gee, Gwyther and Street were grand.'**

I suppose the last thing to say about the afternoon was that once the players left the field and returned to the dressing room they problems were not over. When the players went to get a hot shower to not only clean up but also get warm they found the water was stone cold! It would appear the hot water system was not working properly.

It must also be noted at this point that what was getting lost in all the many thousands of words written of the game was that the Australians had played just as well as the visitors. As a result, the Ashes were not lost or won by either outfit following the first encounter.

On the Wednesday the disputed try by Holland was once more brought to the fore when film from both Movietone and Cinesound was released. The results were inconclusive but seemed to support the referee's decision. The film showed Holland and Ashcroft contesting for the ball it was followed by the sight of the ball under Holland's right arm or body. What cannot be seen is if he actually touched the ball or not as the view is blocked by an English player coming into the shot. We then see the ball moving away from Holland.

The referee George Bishop stated:-

"At no time did Holland contact the ball on the ground with his hand. The laws of the game provide that a try is gained by the player who first puts his hand on the ball in his opponent's in-goal."

The English player for their part strongly believed that no try had been scored. Ratcliffe told the reporters that Holland had missed the ball and he had then kicked it over the try line and touched it down. It was a view that Ward supported when questioned.

There was little time to celebrate the victory as on the Wednesday the tourists were to face North Coast up in Kempsey north of Sydney. They went by train with the intention of playing the game and then continuing the journey up to Brisbane in Queensland. The game took on added significance for two of the players, Daniels the winger who had recovered from an ankle injury was the first. The second was prop Featherstone who had not played since hurting a knee in the first game over in Perth was also selected to play. Good games would bring both of them into contention for a spot in the second Test.

Sadly, the tourists had problems even before the game due to a mix up over accommodation for the tour party. Tom Spedding the manager was under the impression that the players would be housed in a sleeper carriage as part of the Brisbane train. The local authorities were also of that opinion but the Station Master at Kempsey knew nothing about the arrangements. The local authorities quickly arranged hotel accommodation for some of the players with others being accommodated in private houses in the town. While not ideal Spedding made light of the issue telling the reporters, **"Dunkirk was much worse than this!"**

Unfortunately for the visitors the difficulties did not stop there. The game was played in front of around 6,500 local supporters yet another 'record' crowd for the area. It was a game that the Englishmen won going away by 37-7 but as is always the case disaster is only a tackle away. Sadly, that proved to be the case for the winger Arthur Daniels. The winger was running hard for the line when he was tackled from behind and fell awkwardly on his shoulder which resulted in a broken collar bone. It seems incredible that both left wingmen should be out of action with almost the same type of injury. Pollard had it was found dislocated a collar bone now his team mate had broken his.

On the upside Featherstone seemed to have come through the game unscathed and played very well actually scoring a try in the first half. Horne and Pepperell had blended well as the half back pair. In truth they operated together much better than Williams and Bradshaw had particularly in the first Test. The problem was that Williams and Bradshaw had never played together before coming on tour. Williams was a Welshman while Bradshaw was English. The other pleasing aspect was the form shown by Ledgard at full back for while all felt he would not displace Ryan at full back Ledgard was not of that opinion.

On the down side of the game other than the injury to Daniels was the problems encountered with the referee. There were a great many penalties against the visitors and many in the crowd felt the referee was being lenient regarding forward passes. Many times, he gave a scrum when the rule locally was that it should have resulted in a penalty. Both the managers were more than a little concerned with the refereeing of games particularly when they left the city. It was a worry that would prove to be very well founded as the tourists moved up into Queensland where they would face yet more differing local interpretations of the same set of rules.

When the tourists left Kempsey by train bound for Brisbane they left Daniels behind in the local hospital for treatment on the collar bone, he would rejoin the party later. There was however a growing discontent within the tour party a discontent that was not helped by the actions of the two managers. Amongst the players there was a growing belief that there were two teams in the party. There was the so-called Test team and then the second team. The press were beginning to make comments about this very issue. There was also a concern among the players that George Oldroyd was at times 'missing in action'. Even at this stage of the tour he had not been seen at matches. When the team to face Queensland on the Saturday was announced it did little to dispel the notion the players had of there being two teams in the party. Jim Ledgard and Jim Featherstone were not in the team even after play so well and Featherstone really needed to play games also Horne was selected to partner Bradshaw.

CHAPTER FOUR

(Tour derailed, Test match lost, manager in trouble)

In Brisbane excitement was growing to such a pitch that the authorities were confident that the record crowd of 22,500 that witnessed the 1946 game would easily be beaten. There was little rest for the tourists who were to face a very strong Queensland side on the Saturday and were experiencing something of an injury crisis. With both left wingmen out there was now concern over the skipper Ward who had injured his back in the first Test and aggravated it in the game at Kempsey. In Brisbane the tourists were given the news that the second Test for the first time ever was to be an 'all-ticket' affair. Even at this early stage the authorities had sold 34,000 with only one thousand tickets remaining.

On the Saturday the tourists were quite confident, after all they were as yet undefeated on the tour. They had selected a strong side and were confident they could maintain their winning run. At the back of the mind of both managers was the thought that here in Queensland the referees were going to play a big part in matches. Under a cloudy sky on a warm afternoon the two teams took to the field in front of some 22,000 spectators. The managers had a change of heart and decided to play Featherstone at prop for the game. They also put Horne in at stand off to see if he could strike up a better understanding with Bradshaw than was the case with Williams. The team was:-

Ryan, Ratcliffe, Ward, Ashcroft, Hilton, Horne Bradshaw, Gee, Egan, Featherstone, Ryan, Higgins, Street.

The game did not start well for the visitors, early on Ryan was caught off side and the penalty gave Queensland a lead of 2-0. When Bradshaw tackled a player after he had kicked it resulted in yet another two points and a 4-0 lead. Things went from bad to worse when Ratcliffe in making a strong run down the touch line was injured in the resulting tackle and carried from the field. Street was pulled out of the pack to play on the wing when the game resumed. The Queensland pack was at times out playing the tourist forwards with two and three forwards going in to tackle man and ball to stifle the English backs.

Somewhat against the run of play Gee took the ball up in a ruck and with a surprising degree of agility for a big man beat two defenders. As he came to the full back the ever-supporting Hilton was on his side and took a pass. There was no one who could get near the speedy wingman who ran around behind the post for a try that Ward converted and the visitors were in front 4-5. The lead was short lived when the Queensland stand off Andrews scored probably one of the most spectacular tries seen at that ground.

Collecting the ball on the outside of the scrum Andrews broke through a gap and ran fully seventy-yard pass Englishman after Englishman. When he neared the full back Ryan he put in a clever kick towards the try line. The turning Ryan was never going to recover his ground and Andrews coolly regathered the ball over the line to score a great three pointer. Sadly, Linde who had earlier been so reliable with the boot hit the upright with the conversion attempt but his team lead 7-5.

Linde made amends a few minutes later slotting over his third penalty to stretch the lead out to 9-5. The visiting forwards now started to get their game together and in the home twenty-five yard area combined to get the next score. Higgins won the ball at a ruck and quickly fed it out to Egan, he in turn passed on to Gee in support. Gee held up the ball long enough to attract the defence and slipped out a peach of a pass to his prop team mate Featherstone. There was no stopping the big prop as he carried two defenders over the try line with him for a converted try and the lead once more at 9-10.

The English were now seemingly constantly on the attack helped considerable by Egan who at this stage had won the scrums 16 to 6. From a scrum the referee called out Gee and his opposite number and gave both a talking too but the penalty went to Queensland and Linde saw his kick hit the post but this time it bounced in over the cross bar to give his team the lead 11-10. That remained the score as the teams ended the half Egan may well have been winning the scrums with ease but the Englishmen were on the losing end of a twelve to three penalty count from the referee.

In the dressing room the skipper Ward gave vent to his feelings telling the players they needed to play much better. They were in truth a far cry from the side that had triumphed in the first Test in Sydney. The second half began much as the first had this time it was a penalty for a play the ball infringement that saw Linde kick his fifth penalty to take the lead out to 13-10. The English hit back when Bradshaw broke through from a scrum and once clear passed to Street who looked certain to score. Linde covered across and tackled Street at the try line. The English players leapt into the air thinking a try had been scored only to see the referee disallow the score claiming Street had made a double movement. The skipper Ward went up to the referee to ask him about his decision but the try was still disallowed.

The game was now getting a little rougher but it was the home side who were on the wrong end of the penalties and Ward slotted over two in reasonably quick succession to give the tourists the lead once more 13-14. At this time the touch judges seemed to be running onto the field with monotonous regularity reporting one infringement after another. The home side were defending as if their lives depended on it and the feelings on both sides began to run very high. The tourists could not get the break through they were looking for and when the touch judge ran on yet again the referee penalized the tourists and up strode Linde to slot over his sixth penalty goal to take the score to 15-14.

With play deep in the Queensland half both packs squared up to each other and it looked like a brawl would ensue but the referee stepped in quickly and calmed matters down. Sadly, when the referee blew the final whistle a brawl did ensue over the touch line. Bradshaw had tackled a player as the whistle sounded. He then dumped him to the ground and pushed his face into the ground. Players from both sides ran in and a melee ensued. The referee and some of the players broke up the brawl and the tour manager George Oldroyd raced to the touch line and escorted Bradshaw away to the dressing room.

The winning run of the tourists was over and they were beaten for the first time on the tour. Many felt that their cause had not been helped by the referee who had awarded some twenty six penalties against them while only awarding them ten. As they left the field the crowd cheered their own while booing the tourists. There is little doubt that a great deal of fists, elbows and boots were used on both sides and yet the referee while heavily penalizing the visitors saw fit not to send one player from the field. Perhaps if he had the game would have settled down and players got on with playing rugby, who knows.

The referee came in for criticism from the likes of Harry Sunderland who felt that strong personalities were needed to referee such matches. The need was to identify over vigorous play before it descended into violent play. Sunderland revealed that the previous season over in

England the authorities sent out special circulars to all referees asking them to discriminate between hard play and dirty play. This was always denied by the authorities in England but Sunderland felt that dirty play needed to be stamped out particularly by the home sides if the Ashes were to be won. From the English point of view the fears they had regarding local referees was in their minds proving to be correct and growing ever more by the day.

After the game Ward the skipper remained silent preferring to keep his own council with regard to the performance of referee Johnny Hoffman. However, in an interview with Bill Corbett on the Monday he broke his silence on the referee and his display.

"I am not squealing but I went up to the referee on Saturday, quite a lot of times and asked him why he was penalizing us.
He replied 'I am refereeing this game-penalty against you.'
A referee who lets go what this referee did on Saturday, is not fit to be in charge. If he had taken a firm grip on the game it would have been a grand match."

Ward went on to say what many people had been saying since the very first tour back in 1908 that countries need to get together and arrive at a common interpretation of the rules for international games or the problems will continue. Certainly, the referee came in for criticism from some reporters for not sending off a couple of players during the game. They felt it was his leniency that almost led to an all-out brawl as the game was coming to an end.

The worries the two managers had with regard to the refereeing of their matches were shown to be not without foundation. In an effort to arrive at a solution they contacted the Australian Board and requested that for the second Test in Brisbane that they be allowed to select the referee from New South Wales match officials. The practice back then was for the hosts to submit three referees to the tour managers and they would then select the referee they would like to handle the Test match.

The argument put forward by the managers that they had not had enough time in Queensland to see referees officiating in their games to make a decision as to who should handle the Test match. The New South Wales members of the Board deliberated and then contacted their counterparts north of the border. They then refused the tour managers request and stated that the system in operation for a number of years should be maintained. The result was that the names of three Queensland referees would be submitted as in the past. The decision filled the tour party with foreboding as past experience showed that Brisbane had been their undoing on more than one occasion.

It was revealed that such was the depth of feeling toward the performance of Hoffman in the Queensland game that both Spedding and Oldroyd wrote again to the Australian Board and also to the Queensland authorities asking that they not submit Hoffman as a Test choice referee. They went even further and requested that he not referee any further games involving the tourists in Queensland. The authorities refused both requests and Hoffman was submitted as a possible Test referee along with Ballard and Reithmuller. This particularly angered the managers as in effect they were being given a choice of only two officials. They had also asked the Australian Board if the two referees Ballard and Reithmuller could each be assigned one of the tourist games before the second Test in order that the managers could see them in action. Sadly, the request was denied as the claim was that local officials had already been appointed to those games. As a result, the managers were forced to select 'blind' for the Test match with disastrous consequences for the game in general and the tourists in particular as we shall see.

The tour however had to go on and all the controversy was felt left behind in Brisbane as the tourists travelled up to Townsville. Sadly, that proved not to be the case but this time the controversy was off the field. When the players arrived in Townsville they found the accommodation not to their liking. Some were sleeping in beds on the hotel verandah. The players complained to the managers but as was pointed out in order to accommodate all the tour party at one hotel as had been requested this was the only solution. The players simply got on with the job at hand the game against North Queensland to be played on the Wednesday. George Oldroyd however had stored up his resentment at the situation for a later date.

At the official reception in Townsville the manager George Oldroyd got himself into hot water not for the first time on the tour and certainly not for the last time either when he rose to respond to one of the toasts. In his response he said :-

"If you want to learn all the finer points of the game, you have a good man in Brisbane, Professor Hoffman. I don't want to dwell on the Professor any longer, we shall deal with him before we leave your shores."

It was an unfortunate choice of words but does show the depth of feeling both he and the rest of the tour party had with regard to just how the Queensland game had been handled by the referee. Little did he know at that time that worse was to come, far worse. However, given he was the business manager such criticism should really have come from the team manager Tom Spedding.

If that were not bad enough Oldroyd took umbrage at Jack Reardon the reporter from the Sydney Sunday Mail. Reardon had been at the reception when Oldroyd spoke and consequently reported what had been said. Oldroyd in a fit of pique banned the reporter from the rest of the Australian leg of the tour. Such a move was only going to put the newspapers further off side with him and the players.

The players on the other hand enjoyed greatly training in the warm sunshine in Townsville and also the warmth of the welcome offered to them by the local rugby fans who came along to watch the training. They had accepted the somewhat unusual accommodation provided for them and got on with trying to get some rest and also get over the boredom of the long train journeys they were enduring.

The game against North Queensland had a little more added significance for the tourists not least as they had only one recognized wingman to choose from as Hilton's badly sprained ankle had turned out to be worse than first feared and the second Test was looming ever closer. The experiment of playing Danby on the left wing was resurrected once more, this time with spectacular results. The game was won against a very strong side by 39-18 and Danby contributed two spectacular tries. There were other successes to give the managers further selection headaches.

Dickie Williams had an outstanding game and must have surely played himself into contention for the second Test. The problem was that whenever he played with Bradshaw the pair never really seemed to gel. He thrived on the early service he received from his scrum half Pepperell and simply outplayed his opposite number the Aussie stand-off Andrews. The other great success was

Jim Ledgard the fullback. His play albeit considered by many to be 'outmoded' compared to the approach of Martin Ryan was outstanding and must also have given the managers food for thought with regard to the Test.

The Sydney Morning Herald carried a little piece following the game that beggar's belief. They wrote of one person at the game:-

"Bernie Brown a Tobruk veteran with a war damaged leg. He had persuaded the hospital authorities to postpone the amputation of his leg for a few days so that he could see England play the team which he had helped to choose while in hospital."

There are fans of the game and then there are fans of the game and then again there is Bernie Brown.

The tourists once again went to the railway station and a train up to Rockhampton where they were to play Central Queensland on the Sunday. While in Rockhampton preparing for the game Spedding and Oldroyd received a request from officials up in Cairns to play a game against Cairns on the following day the Monday. The offer was to fly the thirteen up to Cairns and then fly them back the same day. An extra incentive was that the tourists would keep all of the gate money. The request was turned down as the need it was felt was to preserve the players for the vital second Test.

The game turned out to be a training run for the tourists as they ran away from the home side winning 88-0.

Sadly, as is ever the case even in such an easy game, injuries occur and the curse of the wingmen struck once more. After just twenty-five minutes Gordon Ratcliffe suffered a bruised shin and Tom Spedding the manager ordered him to come off the pitch and he took no further part in the match. The other injury was to Doug Phillips who damaged a rib cartilage, he was strapped up and continued for most of the game. Once again Tom Danby playing on the wing did himself no harm by crossing for five tries, utility Jack Cunliffe also crossed for four tries in the twenty try rout.

Following the game speculation was rife as to who was to play in the Test match. Indications were given as it was noted that the Test players would fly back to Brisbane to prepare for the big game with the rest returning by train via Gympie and a mid-week game. Willie Horne who had kicked nine goals in the rout was on the airplane and all felt it would be him not Williams who would be pulling on the stand-off jersey come the Saturday.

(*'There is an interesting story in the Brisbane newspaper with regard to Horne that shows I suppose that there is nothing new in this game. It is widely believed that John Gray when he signed for Wigan was the first to use the round the corner style of goal kicking with the side of the foot. The Telegraph published a photograph of Horne kicking and talked of his unusual style of kicking with the inside of his foot claiming it gave him greater accuracy.'*)

There were other issues to be sorted out as well and that was reflected in the team that was to meet Wide Bay and Burnett League on that Wednesday. The team selected was:-

Ledgard, Ratcliffe, Cunliffe, Street, Danby, Williams, Pepperell, Featherstone, Osmond, Haughton, Murphy, Ryan, Traill.

With both Ward and Ashcroft suffering from niggling injuries they were not considered. Ratcliffe was tentatively selected to play in order to see if he had recovered from the knock in the previous game. Danby was to play as the feeling was the more experience he could get playing on the wing the better. Featherstone was also to play as he was considered to be a bit short of match time and if he was to make the Test team he needed a good performance. The other interesting selection was that of Street at centre the speedy forward it was felt would not be out of place at this level. Street had actually begun his career with St. Helens who signed him as a youngster as a centre.

Down in Sydney the tourists would have been pleased to receive the news that the matches planned for the Sydney Cricket Ground had been switched to the Sports Ground. The reason for this was that the almost continual rain in Sydney since the tourists left had seen the ground in a waterlogged state. It was felt if the ground was to be in good condition for the thirst Test it would greatly benefit from the rest. As for the game at

Gympie once again it was Tom Danby who stole the show in yet another 84-9 rout. On this occasion he topped his efforts in the previous game crossing this time for six tries to become the top try scorer in the party. The prop Featherstone also turned in a great performance albeit against poor opposition but must have played himself into a Test spot.

Back in Brisbane it was announced that Frank Ballard had been selected by the tourists to referee the second Test. In truth the managers were faced with 'Hobson's Choice' given they had not seen him or Reithmuller officiate at any game. Also, the team to contest that second Test was not announced until after a training session on the Friday morning. On that morning as the players went about their work Tom Spedding, George Oldroyd, Ernest Ward and Joe Egan were seen deep in discussion on the touch line. Finally, the team was announced to the players and then to the press. There was to be three changes from the first encounter against the green and gold. The reporters were once again less than happy with the announcement of the Test team. They felt that by delaying the notification of the team until Friday it gave them little time to report on the team and to build up excitement for the game. It was a problem they faced on many occasions on this tour. The selection was not the only matter that needed to be addressed in the week leading to the Test.

When the Australian team was announced and four changes were made the pressmen were scathing of the actions of the selection. Many felt that it hinted at panic after all they had only just lost in the first Test on a mud bath of a pitch. The English players and managers were asked for their opinions and politely stated that one or two of the selection mystified them. If that was the serious stuff the next was pure farce as Tom Spedding had to deny in the press that the tourists intended to take a 'dive' in the Brisbane Test. The story was that by doing so and leveling the series a bumper crowd would be assure in the final encounter in Sydney. Spedding told reporters the main priority of the tour was to return home with the Ashes and to win them as soon as possible.

When Spedding gave the team for the second Test to the press it also showed a number of changes, three in fact. It had been decided that while Ryan the full back seemed to be returning to something like his best form after a poor spell, Ledgard had earned his chance at full back. That would entail a slight change of role for the scrum half Bradshaw. When Ryan was at full back Bradshaw would run back to support Ryan who always ran the ball back rather than kicking for position and his forwards. Now with Ledgard he had no need to retreat and help his full back out.

In conversation with Jack Hilton he had told the managers he was only 90% recovered from the ankle injury. On that basis it was decided not to risk him and Tom Danby was to get the wing berth. The biggest shock was in the pack, as it was widely expected that Jim Featherstone would occupy one of the prop positions, with Gwyther dropping to the second row to accommodate him. In actual fact Featherstone was not selected and Harry Murphy was selected in the second row. Murphy would make his Test debut despite the fact he had toured Australia four years earlier with Risman's squad. He was considered a no nonsense, no frills player ideally suited for the hard graft needed up front.

There were two other issues in the camp that were causing some concern the first was the continuing resentment that was building up in the players with regard to the growing belief that there were actually two teams in the squad the Test thirteen and the mid-week thirteen. One newspaper when writing of a game in the north of Queensland had referred to the England team that took to the field as the 'Great Britain second team'. This had particularly upset a number of the players.

The other issue was a nagging worry in the back of the mind of the managers and the captain and vice-captain. The last three games had been won with a great deal of ease and high scores run up. However, another high score had been run up namely the number of penalties referees were awarding against them. In the main the penalties were being conceded either at the play the ball or in the scrum. The English were used to dropping the ball behind their foot at the play the ball but the Australian players were made to drop the ball in front of the foot. One rule two totally different interpretations! The second was the way in which the English scrum half was feeding the ball into the scrum.

Tommy Bradshaw in particular had incurred the wrath of many of the officials who insisted that the ball be fed in the scrum underarm and rolled on the floor. Bradshaw was used to feeding the scrum standing up and throwing the ball in with a downward motion. Often, he would bounce the ball of the back of Joe Egan's leg as the pair of them worked the scrums back home for Wigan. The feeling was growing that if the referee was to inflict a similar penalty count on the team then it was going to be difficult to win the Test match. Sadly, all of the fears were to come to fruition.

On that Friday morning the Englishmen went to the Cricket ground for a light training run and a loosening up. They were more than a little perturbed at the condition of the cricket square in the middle of the pitch. It was crusted and corrugated and the players felt it was an accident waiting for players who were tackled or tackling in that area. After talking to the groundsman it was agreed that the area would be watered and then rolled. It was hoped this would solve the problem come Saturday afternoon. The other problem concerned the stand off Horne who it was revealed had quite a serious Achilles injury and he had not been considered for the Test.

On the Saturday afternoon at 2.30 pm. the two teams that took to the field were:-

Australia:-

Churchill, Flannery, Andrews, Middleton, Graves, Stanmore, Holman, Thompson, Schubert, Holland, Crocker, De Belin, Cowie.
England:-
Ledgard, Ratcliffe, Ward, Ashcroft, Danby, Williams, Bradshaw, Gee, Egan, Gwyther, Murphy, Higgins, Street.

When the game kicked off the Englishmen had won the previous six encounters and it looked for all the world they were likely to make it seven. Early in the game Churchill collected a kick from Ledgard and returned it down on Tom Danby's side of the field. Tommy Bradshaw collected the ball and sprinted up to the advancing Australian defence. When he passed to Danby there was nothing on or so it appeared. Danby proceeded to weave a swathe through the defenders and beat them with ease. Once clear he simply ran around Churchill to score out wide. Sadly, Ward could not add on the extra two but the visitors were leading 0-3.

A few minutes later Ashcroft worked a little magic of his own and got free on the left wing. He cleared his own twenty-five yard area and as he approached the ten yard line he had Danby in support. His pass out was ruled to be forward by the referee Ballard who penalized the Englishmen for being off side. From forty yard out, Graves stepped up and nailed the penalty to take the score to 2-3. It was a penalty that irked the tourists who felt the correct decision would have been to award a scrum.

It was obvious to all on the ground just how important the match was to both sides as the players were tense and errors were occurring as a result. Later in the half the referee was to influence the game greatly not for the last time. Danby who was having the game of his life got the ball and simply bumped off the tackle of his opposite number Flannery to streak into the clear. With the cover coming across he stopped and passed the ball inside to Ashcroft who immediately passed on to Williams. Williams had no one in front of him and no Australian player within yards and a try seemed obvious. It was then the whistle went and the referee ruled the pass forward. The problem was that the referee was some twenty yards behind the play but he somehow ruled the ball had gone forward.

The tourists were then on the wrong end of five consecutive penalty and all the momentum they were building was halted. Inevitably it was the home side that were to score and a cracking try it was. Andrews collected a pass and looking up saw Graves on the wing was free his pin point accurate kick for the corner seemed to be under control but Ratcliffe was a little too casual in getting to the ball. Williams came across to assist and appeared to confuse Ratcliffe who misjudged the bounce of the ball. Graves did not and as he collected the bouncing ball he ran on through to score in the corner.

The conversion was missed but with just three minutes left in the half the home side had the lead 5-3 much against the run of play in the first half. The second stanza saw a good deal of heavy tackling from both sides in what was turning into a blood and guts Test match typical of games between the two sides. With Danby and Williams on the touch line receiving treatment following heavy tackles the referee awarded another penalty which Holland the prop forward banged over to stretch the home sides lead to 7-3. It was half way into the half that the referee really turned the game on its head.

Ashcroft intercepted a pass and shot for the line and as Churchill tackled him just short of the line he hit the ground and his momentum bounced him over the line. Ballard sadly saw it differently and ruled a double movement cancelling the try out. Ashcroft threw the ball away in disgust, but Bradshaw who was up in support said something to the referee who promptly sent him from the field to the disgust of the tourists. Worse was to follow for the visitors just a couple of minutes later when Egan made a great break and raced away down the field. He had Williams on his inside in support and when he got to Churchill he passed the ball to him. As Williams was sprinting away to the line the whistle blew and Ballard ruled once again the ball had gone forward. Gee was absolutely furious and vented his feelings close by the referee. Ballard once again reached for his whistle and promptly marched Gee for an early bath.

The tourists were now permanently down to eleven men and there was around sixteen minutes of the match to go. Try as they may they faced an uphill battle against the

Aussies and the extra effort simply took its toll. The stand off Stanmore made a break and passed out to Cowie a pass that many on the ground thought was forward but the referee did not and the converted try took the score to 12-3 and the game away from the Englishmen. With the game in its dying stages Holman broke away and seemingly scored in the corner, as the referee pointed to the spot Danby held up the ball the implication being he had robbed Holman of the ball before he could touch down. The try stood and the Test was lost 15-3.

It was a very disappointed English dressing room following the game not least because they had they felt once again been robbed by a Queensland referee. The managers and the skipper Ward made their feelings known and were of course well aware that their words could be considered a case of sour grapes. Fortunately, many of the Australian reporters in writing of the game seemed to support the Englishmen's point of view. Len Smith in the Sunday Sun was incensed:-

"Refereeing of the match was the worst I have ever seen. The Englishmen lost the game in the first half when referee Frank Ballard disallowed a try between the posts by English five-eight Dickie Williams.
In my opinion it was a fair try, Ashcroft throwing the ball inside to Williams who was behind him.
I was directly opposite the play and was probably in a better position than Ballard who was 30 yards behind the ball.

Ballard ruled a forward pass.
The other disputed try came when Ashcroft was tackled near the line by Churchill. Ballard ruled that Ashcroft had made two movements with the ball and penalized him.
To me this was also a fair try.
Churchill tackled Ashcroft side on and Ashcroft who was running strongly was not effectively stopped. His momentum carried him over the line."

Smith went on to list other events when the referee had not penalized the Australians for such things as not facing the goal line when playing the ball. He claimed on many occasions the Australians were standing off side but not penalized. As he wrote of Ballard. **'However, he was one sided and Australia offended on several occasions without being penalized.'**

Sadly, immediately following the game Oldroyd was to once more upset the press. When he was entering the dressing-room he slammed the door in the face of one newsman trying to get to speak to the players. Once inside he saw a reporter already in the room and promptly ordered him from the room. His rude behavior was not lost on the reporters.

On the Monday Bill Corbett writing in the Sun revealed that the skipper Ward had been threatened with an early bath by the referee. When Bradshaw had been sent from the field Ward approached the referee and asked him to watch the Australians as they were infringing in the scrums without being penalized. Ballard told him if he were not careful he would be the next to be sent off! Corbett was scathing also of the performance of the referee:-

"These refereeing controversies occur too frequently here. I have seen refereeing in England, France and New Zealand as well as in Australia. Saturday's display was the most deplorable I have observed.'

Corbett also revealed some of the thoughts of the players following the controversial defeat they included such things as cancelling next Thursday's game against Brisbane. Many felt that Queensland did not want the tourists to play games in the state. Some players went so far as to eliminate playing games in Queensland on future tours instead playing the strong club sides in Sydney. Finally, one player told him he wished he could travel home tomorrow. It was shocking stuff but it all went over the head of the referee Frank Ballard.

He was unrepentant about his control of the game and the controversy his decisions had caused. He accused the tourists of being 'squealers' which did not sit well with the players. He also claimed that he had sent off both Bradshaw and Gee for using foul and abusive language to him. It was a claim both players denied vehemently Bradshaw stated that all he said was 'sliding try sir' and was promptly sent off. Gee claimed he had sworn but not directly to the referee but his comments had been over heard by Ballard resulting in him also getting an early bath.

It would be fair at this point to make the comment that all of the reports mentioned were taken from newspapers based in New South Wales. Those making the comments were either well respected rugby league reporters or former Australian international players well versed in the game. When you look at the newspaper reports from Brisbane a totally different picture emerges. There is little or no criticism of the Queensland based referee and they all seemed to stress the justification for his sending off the two tourists. I suppose it is a good example of the inter state rivalry that existed then in reporting and no doubt still exists today.

The sad thing was that all the controversy that filled the column inches of the newspapers took the shine off what was a very good victory by the green and gold. They had contained a very good English back line, held their own with the pack and out scored the tourists. All of that seemed to have got lost in the criticism of Ballard. If the authorities felt that the controversy was going to fade away the Queensland authorities saw to it that it would not when they held a disciplinary hearing on the Monday.

At the hearing the big issue was that neither Bradshaw or Gee had been issued a caution before they had been dismissed from the field. The other area of dissention came when the referees report was that the players had used foul language, he claimed on disallowing the Ashcroft try Bradshaw had called him 'A f****** Pirate' a claim both the player and the managers denied. He also claimed Gee had abused him in a similar manner. Gee in his defence stated he had made comments but they were to his own players rather than the referee.

When the hearing ended the Queensland authorities at the disciplinary meeting appeared to shoot themselves in the foot. They suspended Bradshaw for two matches but simply issued a caution to Gee and no suspension. The press had a field day with that decision and what came out of the hearing. The English skipper Ward was under no illusions as to just why Bradshaw had been suspended and said so to the press:-

"Suspension of half back Tommy Bradshaw for two matches was described today by England's rugby league captain Ernest Ward as 'a cover up' for referee Frank Ballard."

Bradshaw was upset not only at being sent from the field for the first time in his career but also by the treatment he received at the hearing as he related to Bill Corbett in the Sun:-

"Bradshaw told me last night, other matters were gone into concerning previous matches such as putting the ball into the scrums. These matters had nothing whatsoever to do with the allegations over Saturdays match. Bradshaw added 'I did not use the

words attributed to me in Ballard's report. My suspension was a great shock.'"

It is also worth noting that he was the first tourist to be suspended while on an Australian tour yet another first he would rather not have had.

There is no doubt that the whole incident left a nasty taste in the mouth for every rugby league supporter and official both in Australia and over in the north of England. The only people seemingly oblivious to events were the Queensland authorities and the referee Frank Ballard. While all this kerfuffle was being aired in the newspapers the tour simply had to go on and go on it did. There is no doubt whatsoever that the events of the second Test left the tourists deflated, dispirited and down hearted and would affect them for the rest of the tour.

On the 4th July the tourists were in Toowoomba to face the local side. While not the strength they once were Toowoomba were something of a banana skin for the visitors particularly given the ongoing saga over the second Test. The result was a relatively easy win by 44-12. The wingman Tom Danby seemed not to be suffering any hangover from the Test as he sped in for four tries one of them a beauty from seventy-five yard out when he bamboozled the Toowoomba players completely. Sadly, the curse of the wingmen struck once more with Ratcliffe pulling a muscle not in one leg but both! On the plus side Featherstone was continuing to show the sort of form that earned him a place on the tour.

It was then back to Brisbane to meet the Brisbane side and there was undoubtably a great deal of resentment in the party as they prepared to meet Brisbane on that Thursday. Over 12,000 turned up hoping for a repeat of the Test win but the visitors were in no mood for that. The game was started by the Premier of Queensland Mr. Hanlon and it did not take long for the tourists to go ahead when Ward slotted over an easy penalty. Featherstone quickly consolidated the lead by using his strength to barge over for a try Ward again added the extras two and a 7-0 lead.

It was then that the whistle began to sound once again with monotonous regularity as scrum and play the ball offences against the visitors were spotted by the referee. From one the Brisbane team got on the score board but Ward responded by putting over a magnificent fifty-yard penalty of his own to make the score 11-2. At the half time break the penalty count against the Englishmen stood at 13 to 5. The players were familiar with the story and simply kept their heads down.

The second half saw only scores from penalty goals from either side. If the first half penalty count had been bad, the second half was worse with twenty-two going against the tourist. The game was won however, 18-8 and as the players left the field, they were grateful that no one had been dismissed or injured. The players were now beginning to feel the effects of a punishing game schedule coupled with long train journeys to play those matches. Saturday would see the visitors play their last game in Queensland against Ipswich and it could not come quick enough for the players and managers. All felt it had been a very sad visit to the northern state and not one they ever wished to repeat.

On the Saturday the managers were forced to turn out a makeshift set of backs while the pack was a relatively strong one. Street was once again forced to play on the wing and on the other Hilton made a comeback after his long ankle injury. The other player coming back was the scrum half Tommy Bradshaw having completed his two-match ban. Also, the full back Ryan had been pushed up to play in the centre alongside Street. However, in a somewhat crass decision the authorities had allocated the game to John Hoffman who had been in charge of the Queensland game which had seen the tourists lose for the first time on tour. Neither the managers or the players were happy with the decision Oldroyd in particular was quick to make his feelings known.

Hoffman who had been severely criticized for his handling of that match was closely watched by all the press reporters covering the game. When the game began it was Naughton who wore the prop's jersey Featherstone being pulled out suffering from a foot injury. It was the visitors who drew first blood when the stand off Cunliffe took a pass from Ward and very cleverly slipped a pass out to Street. He ran clear and went behind the posts for the touchdown. Ward converted and the visitors were in the lead 5-0.

It was Cunliffe once again who put his side into an attacking position speeding down field only to be tackled but as he was falling, he fed the ball to Street. As the cover defence came across Street cleverly kicked in field. The covering Ipswich player knocked the ball on over the try line and a scrum was awarded. From the scrum Cunliffe brilliantly scooped up a pass round his ankles and dived in for the second converted try and a 10-0 lead after just fifteen minutes of the game. The try of the game came as the half was coming to a close when the ball passed through eight pairs of hands before Bob Ryan used Hilton as a foil and bamboozled everyone with a dummy and waltzed across for a try.

The Ipswich pack were giving their opposite numbers a torrid time but the tourists continually fed off the mistakes they made. Ryan was next to score and then it was the turn of Gwyther to need the attention of the ambulance men. He damaged a shoulder and was off the field for a time. Early in the second half it was the other prop Naughton who was in the wars when he suffered what was thought to be a leg fracture. The problems did not end there either.

While the first half had been relatively incident free the second half was a different story. With the score at 18-11 to the visitors, thing started to get a bit heated. In one skirmish Harry Murphy let fly with a left hook at his opposite number. The crowd in their excitement had begun encroaching onto the pitch and the referee Hoffman stopped the game and ordered the police to clear supporters from the touchline. When play restarted it appears that Joe Egan borrowed a technique from Dougie Greenall as he launched himself completely off the ground and curled into a ball, at the loose forward and flattened him.

A short time later the forwards from both sides were involved in a melee which saw the touch judge run onto the field. Following his report, the referee called Gwyther over and sent him from the field for indiscriminate kicking. In his defence Gwyther stated he was about to kick the ball when a player dived onto it and so he kicked the player. Given what had gone on before in the State the writing was on the wall for the Welsh prop. In the end the tourist won a very tough encounter 18-13 and with that ended the Queensland leg of the tour. Sadly, the controversy was not yet over.

On the day of the game newspapers carried reports from the Rugby League officials in the North of England which were critical of George Oldroyd the English manager feeling his actions were 'tactless'. The Sun reported:-

"League officials believe that tactless statements by British Rugby League team business manager George Oldroyd contributed to dissention over the second Test in Brisbane.
The officials also claimed that forthright statements by English player-writers played a major part in the second Test dispute.

B.B. Mason of Salford Chairman of the Rugby League Press and Publicity Committee and a member of the tour selection committee said. 'Players are sent out to play and managers to manage. Leave reporting of matches to professional journalists.'
Rugby League Secretary Bill Fallowfield confirming that players won't be allowed to write in future, said. 'Australian Chairman Jersey Flegg is wrong in saying we have been misled by reports written by our players. We only act on official reports and none have been received yet on the second Test.'

It was a slap in the face for the English manager by officials back in England and only added fuel to the fire for Queensland officials who claimed it vindicated them. It also fueled the fire of resentment amongst the players who felt they had not received the support from home they deserved. It was all becoming very very messy and vitriolic. The problem was that Oldroyd was dominating the messages sent out to the newspapers while Spedding for whatever reason said very little. He was however coupled with Oldroyd's utterings.

As the tourists prepared to leave for New South Wales the Ipswich disciplinary committee found Gwyther guilty of the charge and suspended him for one game. There was worse news to follow when hospital x-rays clearly showed that the other prop Naughton had indeed broken his leg and he would be out for the rest of the tour. All in all, the tour party as a whole were glad to be heading south. The Queensland authorities were also happy to see them leave but they had not finished with George Oldroyd. The Queensland Rugby League Secretary wrote to his counterpart Bill Fallowfield outlining in the strongest possible terms their displeasure at the behaviour of Oldfield.

CHAPTER 5
(Return to NSW Ashes lost)

The tour party left Brisbane in two groups, one consisting of players the press considered to be Test players along with injured players with Oldroyd flew down to Sydney to prepare for the NSW game. The second group travelled by train down to Gunnedah to play Northern Division. This action simply reinforced a growing belief both within the party and also outside that there were in actual fact two teams, the Test team and the mid-week team. In addition, following all the bad publicity that had been engendered by the injudicious comments both to the press and at official functions by George Oldroyd there was a growing rumour of a split between the two managers that was not going away. The problem was that whatever controversial statement George Oldroyd uttered was attributed by the press to 'the managers', both were being tarred with the same brush! In truth Tom Spedding seems to have said little that was reported by the reporters.

In Sydney concern was growing with regard to the state of the Sydney Cricket Ground as the rains had continued to fall and flooding was an ever present on the ground. On previous tours this news would have been greeted with delight by the tourists. On this tour it generated dismay as the style of play that had been the norm was for fast open football which made best use of the English backs. Also, in Sydney inquiries within the players revealed that it was their opinion that the hard cricket squares were the reason for so many injuries to the players. They were used to being tackled on the softer grounds in England but here many of the cricket squares were as hard as concrete.

Of the eleven players flown to Sydney nine were suffering injuries of varying severity. Trail had both leg and knee injuries, Williams had fluid on the knee and ligament damage. Skipper Ernest Ward had an arm that had become septic while Horne was carrying an Achilles tendon injury. Bob Ryan had a pulled muscle in his leg while the two wingmen Daniels and Pollard were still recovering from collar bone injuries. To add to the woes Ratcliffe the other winger had a groin strain and was unfit. Also, preparations were being made to ship Naughton home if at all possible, as with his broken leg his tour was over.

Meanwhile up in Gunnedah Bradshaw was looking very much out of sorts the cheerful chirpy scrum half seemed to have gone into his shell and the concern was simply would he have recovered from the mauling the referees up in Queensland had subjected him to in time for the now vital third Test. The extend of Bradshaw's disenchantment can be seen in an interview he gave to Bill Corbett:-

"Queensland referees were severer on me than those of Sydney. I am upset, I never tried to play against Ipswich. I am absolutely tied up in the game I cannot help talking. In Sydney we have referees with few

exceptions in interpretations, which are like the referees in England. In England, as long as the half-back makes a downward movement with the ball when he is putting it in the scrum he is alright. In Queensland referees tell me I must throw the ball in so that it hits the floor. But I defy any half-back to hit the floor when two hookers are striking. So, I deliberately threw the ball into the Ipswich forwards feet on Saturday."

It was an amazing claim to make from what was at that time England's premier scrum half. It also shows just how the referees in Queensland were placing their own interpretation on the rules. The refereeing in that second Test had a profound effect on the little scrum half.

The managers were also aware of the effect recent events had on their scrum half and for the game against Northern Division Pepperell was given the job of feeding the scrum. Back in Sydney news came through that Tom McMahon was to referee the game against New South Wales The players were particularly pleased at the news for they like many others held the belief he was at that time the best referee in the world. It was also believed that while very strict he would give them a fair go. on the week-end. The managers were taking no chances after what they had experienced in Queensland and arranged for McMahon to meet with the players so that he could explain to them just how he would be interpreting the rules.

Up in Gunnedah the game was producing yet more problems for the tourists. With the game underway the prop Featherstone was forced off the field with a rib injury. With the game wrapped up the hoodoo that had struck the wingmen on this tour struck once more. Hilton who was coming back from injury was limping badly and Tom Spedding the manager called him off the field reducing the team to just eleven men. The game was won going away as they say at 41-4 and on the plus side Pepperell had the proverbial 'blinder' to put pressure on Bradshaw for the Test jersey.

On the following day with the tour party once more united there was still more wingman news for the pressmen. Pollard who had been out for some time with the dislocated collar bone was cleared to play and it was decided not to rush him back into action. He would not come into contention for the game on the Saturday but would play down in Wollongong the following Wednesday. On the down side wingman Ratcliffe was ordered to bed and placed in isolation suffering from the flu and would not play against New South Wales. It seems the tourists could not keep wingmen fit and healthy whatever they did.

The newspapers had a field day following the game at Gunnedah and speculated that Bradshaw could well be dropped for the final Test. The reason for such speculation was the performance they had witnessed from Pepperell. He had combined well with loose forward Street and his half back partner Jack Cunliffe to terrorize the Northern Division team. Tom Spedding did admit that Pepperell was playing very well, enough to warrant a Test spot. He however, confirmed that Bradshaw would play at the Cricket Ground on Saturday. The other player who seemed to have played himself into a Test spot was Ledgard the full back. His displays up in Queensland had been something of a revelation gone was the kicking and catching full back that had started the tour. He was now mixing up his game and taking a leaf out of Martin Ryan's play book, often running the ball back and setting his three quarters off in attacking positions.

The big worry for the tourists was the continuing bad weather in Sydney and the fact that the New South Wales team were training on the Cricket Ground and churning the surface up. Many were saying the pitch was in a worse state than it had been for the first Test. It was a situation which did not favour the visitors. There was little they could do about the situation and set about their own training at the Coogee Oval. Once again not for the first time the managers were reluctant to name their starting lineup a decision that angered the reporters wanting to file stories for their newspapers. They announced the team would be selected on Friday evening it was a position that did little to help the local reporters and even less to dispel the growing antagonism toward the two managers.

When the managers did release the team there were more than a couple of shocks. They had been hampered simply by the number of injuries players in the party were now carrying. Given Hilton and Ratcliffe were out of contention the managers sprung two surprises by selecting Street on one wing and Pollard on the other. Pollard had not played a game since the 3rd June when he had been injured in the NSW game. Tom Danby would occupy one centre spot the skipper Ward the other. That was forced on the visitors as Ashcroft was still not recovered from the groin strain.

The other big shock was to carry on with the half back combination of Cunliffe and Pepperell that had been so successful mid-week. This only added to the speculation that Bradshaw could well be out of the Test team. Traill was selected at loose forward and was only in that position because Street was out on the wing. Traill had been considered to be the number one choice for loose forward prior to the tour but the performances of Street had forced him out. Ledgard had retained the full back spot in place of Ryan such had been the form he had been showing at that time. Finally, Bob Ryan was replaced by Doug Phillips who would play his first game in the state capital on the tour.

The Sydney Cricket Ground was in such a poor condition that the decision was made to cancel the two warm up games planned. Only the NSW versus Queensland schoolboy game would be played and that in the morning to allow repairs to be carried out on the pitch. The authorities had a big problem with the ground as yet more rain was forecast for Sydney. Such was the amount of rain that had fallen and was still falling that the ground was saturated and could take no more water. The result was that it was lying on top of the ground. The problem was that should the ground be unfit to play on then there was no slack in the tour schedule. They were due to fly to Auckland on the Sunday following the final Test. As it stood if the Test was cancelled then with the score at one Test each the tourists would retain the Ashes yet again. The home authorities were reluctant to let that happen.

True to form on the Saturday the rain was still with the city and the pitch was a quagmire and that was before the players even stepped on the pitch. Any chance of attractive football being played on the field was very remote and the tourists realized as much. They played a game that was alien to that they had attempted to play through out the tour to date and it paid off. From the very first scrummage of the game players were covered in thick black mud making identification almost impossible.

The Englishmen ground out a 10-0 victory with a try and a goal in each half. First it was Gwyther who scored a try to augment a penalty from Ledgard to leave the half time score at 5-0. With just ten minutes gone in the second half the injury hoodoo struck once again. This time it was Ward who was tackled heavily by the full back Churchill. As play went on Ward stayed down flat out on his stomach. When the whistle went teammates rushed to turn him onto his back. The ambulance men worked on him and after a couple of minutes he was able to sit up. He was led from the field and work continued on him on the touchline. The verdict was that he was suffering from a mild concussion and took no further part in the game. The tourists faced a hard slog for thirty minutes with only twelve men. It was Higgins who would clinch the game when from close to the NSW line. He collected the ball and in a swerving run which saw him side step off either foot in treacherous conditions, he crossed for a try. Ledgard managed to lift the heavy ball over the cross bar to make the final score 10-0.

In truth the score did not really reflect the advantage the tourists had throughout the game. They were by far the better team and never looked like losing. In a first on the tour the visitors were on the right side of the penalty count. It would seem that the visit by McMahon to the tourist's camp had proved an inspired move. The referee awarded the first six penalties of the game to the Englishmen! The English had two tries disallowed when Ward was penalized for a double movement and Pollard was brought back for a forward pass. The conditions did not auger well for the tourists with the Test at the same venue just seven days away.

The tourists had only one more game to play before the final Test they were to travel around seventy miles south of Sydney to the steel city of Wollongong. The big question was just what sort of team would they be able to put on the field given the Test was the main priority? Also given the fact that Cunliffe and Pepperell had once more performed well this time in adverse conditions, would they be retained for the Test. It was a decision the managers and the skipper along with vice-captain Egan needed to ponder long and hard over.

The Australian selectors had over the previous week-end announced the team to contest the final Test. To many in the press they had done the unthinkable, having won the second Test to level the series they had changed a winning side. They actually made five changes and one of the changes was to have enormous consequences for the home country. The two wingmen Flannery and Graves were replaced by Roberts and Troy. Andrews the centre was out and his place was taken my McRitchie. In the pack Purcell replaced De Belin and Hall came in for Thompson. Given they knew just what the state of the pitch was going to be perhaps they guessed the type of game that needed to be played to win the Test and with it the Ashes.

The tourists according to the newspapers had at least four positions in the team that were up for grabs. The stand-off and scrum half spots were undecided as was the second row and most problematical who would play on the wings. Did the visitors go with Tommy Bradshaw whom it was though if aggravated by the opposition and irritated by refereeing decisions that went against him tended to fade out of the game. On the other hand, Albert Pepperell had hit a rich vein of form but was untested at the very highest level.

The stand off position was equally problematical, if Bradshaw was at scrum half did you select his Wigan team mate Cunliffe who like Pepperell had hit top form. Or did you take the risk of playing Williams knowing he had not really gelled with Bradshaw all the tour. Cunliffe was the more rugged of the two better able to withstand the physicality associated with a match of this standing. Countering that was the fact Williams was a natural stand off as opposed to Cunliffe's utility status and would perhaps work better with Pepperell should he get the nod.

The managers faced a similar problem on the wing. Hilton had left the field injured up in Gunnedah so was not in the team to play in Wollongong on the Wednesday, did that mean they were saving him for the Test. Ratcliffe was still suffering with the flu and so could probably be ruled out. Pollard was an out and out winger but had only played one game since the beginning of June through injury. With two wingers in Pollard and Hilton available did they go with both at the expense of Tom Danby who had performed exceedingly well on the flank in the Test up in Brisbane.

The second-row position was also causing problems for the managers, Ryan, Higgins, Murphy and Phillips were all fit and playing very well. Did they go for speed or select 'mud-runners' given the predicted state of the ground. While it would be easy to say give the 'mud-runners' the nod, all the tour the visitors had played a fast passing and running game whatever the conditions.

Who ever was selected would do a great job the problem was just what job would be needed on Saturday. One very important decision had been made and that was that the Test would be controlled by Tom McMahon who had been in charge of the New South Wales encounter. The tourists felt he had handled the game well and they understood what he wanted from the players on the pitch.

If the tourists did not have enough problems with decisions to be made on the pitch then the managers surely added to them off the field. It was revealed on the Tuesday that the managers had decided not to attend the farewell dinner organized by the Australian Board for the Saturday evening following the Test match. The decision was seen by many in and outside the newspapers as a snub by the visitors but this notion was ridiculed by the Board Chairman Harry Flegg:-

"It's all wrong the decision was made last Friday to cancel the dinner. The players have too many other send-offs to attend. They leave on Sunday morning for New Zealand and with their packing and goodbye's on Saturday night they won't have time to attend a dinner."

Flegg went on the say that the Sydney Cricket Ground Committee had organized a dinner for Thursday evening and that will give members a chance to say goodbye. It was however a remarkable decision by the managers to forgo a farewell dinner by their hosts and was unprecedented by the present tourists. It simply added to the feelings of resentment against the two people managing the players by many in the game in Australia. It was a decision that raised questions back in England by Council members and supporters alike. The question must be asked, was the strong willed personality of Oldroyd prevailing over the other manager with regard to this decision.

On that same Tuesday there was an article in the Sun that would prove to be very prophetic. While many were critical of the team selected by the green and gold officials the coach Vic Hey was of another opinion and stated in the article:-

"Vic Hey thinks that tall wingman Ron Roberts could win the vital third Test for Australia at the SCG on Saturday."

As we shall see he was absolutely spot on in that prediction.

For the game against Southern Districts in Wollongong the team selected cause eyebrows to be raised not least because seven of those selected were in the running for a Test spot three days later. The team selected was

Ryan, Pollard, Street, Danby, Daniels, Williams, Bradshaw, Gwyther, Osmond, Featherstone, Murphy, Ryan, Traill.

Sadly, the game followed the same route as many of the others once out of the city. They game was lost 18-11 and the visitors were on the wrong side of a lopsided penalty count. Also, for the third time a player was ordered from the field again on the intervention of the touch judge. It was reported to the referee that Bob Ryan had struck an opponent and so he got marched. At the disciplinary hearing that same evening Ryan stated he had been tackled without the ball and had simply pushed the tackler away. The good news was that Ryan was simply reprimanded and was free to play in the Test if selected. The other good news was that Daniels the wingman who had been out also with a collar bone break scored two tries on his comeback. The question was, had he done enough to earn a place in Saturday's Test side.

On the down side the most experienced half back in the squad Willie Horne was struggling with an Achilles tendon injury that had troubled him while on the Queensland leg of the tour. It appeared not to have responded well to treatment and there was a great fear that his tour was also over. Quietly and almost unnoticed by the press the squad was being depleted of players in key areas. There was still five more games to be played down in New Zealand before the players returned home.

The day after the game the two managers seemed still to be edging their bets for when the announced the team for the Test match, they bracketed Bradshaw and Pepperell for the scrum half jumper. They selected Higgins for one of the second-row positions but then bracketed Bob Ryan and Doug Phillips for the other spot. They told the waiting reporters that a decision would be made just before kick off as to just who would play. Given that Cunliffe was to play at stand off it was odds on that Bradshaw would partner him. Sadly, Daniels who had played very well was considered to be too much of a risk for such an important game.

On the eve of the game the Cricket Ground was a hive of activity as lorries loaded with sand were brought to the stadium. It was reported that fifty tons of sand was spread over the pitch in an attempt to counter the cloying clinging black mud that proposed to be the rugby league pitch. Once finished the ground looked more like Bondi Beach that a sports ground. The problem was a simple one, would it do the job it had been brought in to do or not. Come that Saturday afternoon it quickly became obvious to all that it would not.

It was also revealed that there would be a new trophy presented to the winners, a new trophy with an old name. The City Tattersall's Cup first presented in 1928 had been replaced with a brand new gold version. In addition, there was to be a handsome plaque which would serve as a miniature version of the monster sized Courtney Goodwill Trophy that the winners will take away. If that were not enough the Claude Corbett Memorial Trophy would be presented to the winning skipper. The only trophy Ernest Ward was interested in was The Ashes.

On the eve of the Test match there was a very frosty meeting between the two managers and the Australian

Board. As was usual at the end of the tour the two parties got together to discuss the tour as a whole and the problems that had been encountered. There is no doubt that the second Test officiating would have figured high on the agenda. The managers would have been adamant that the top referees and only the top referees be asked to officiate at any future tour games. Almost all the troubles had arisen from referee's in districts and particularly in Queensland, interpreting the rules to what they claim were the local conditions.

On the other side of the coin the Australian Board would have been less than happy with the comments made by both George Oldroyd and various players who were contracted to write for newspapers back home. Their views no doubt would have been supported by comments from the authorities back in England. The decision had been taken that on future tours players would not be allowed to write for newspapers while on tour. The Council had also albeit from a long way away reprimanded Oldroyd for his comments in the press regarding the referee of the Brisbane Test.

There were other issues that rankled not least that the managers had preferred for whatever reason to attend a farewell dinner on the Thursday evening hosted by the Cricket Ground Trust rather than the New South Wales Rugby League. This had been done and the traditional end of tour dinner by the NSWRL had been boycotted for the most spurious of reasons. It was a decision that had not gone down well with the hosts and supporters in

Sydney. There can be little doubt after all this, looking back it was a crass decision and a monumental blunder by the managers and one they needed to defend when they arrived home.

As the Saturday of the vital Test dawned the weather was as it had been for weeks, wet and cold. The gates to the ground were opened at 8.00am and when they did there was already a large crowd waiting to get in and claim a good vantage point to watch the game. When they entered, they would have got a shock as the ground was a bright yellow from the sand strewn over the ground. The warm up games had been cancelled due to the state of the pitch with one exception. The game between NSW and Queensland schoolboys went ahead in the morning and resulted in the home side winning 3-0. Their efforts did nothing to improve the state of the playing surface.

Had the conditions as they were been presented to any other English touring party they would have been looked on with relish. Unfortunately, the present players were of a different ilk, they preferred to run the ball at every opportunity given the quality of their backs. There was little chance that they would be able to do that successfully in this game. When the game kicked off there was little doubt that conditions were marginally worse than those that had greeted the players in the first Test. The sad fact was that given what was at stake for both teams the weather badly effected the attendance only 47,178 had paid to witness the battle.

The teams for this epic encounter were:-

AUSTRALIA:-
Churchill, Roberts, Middleton, McRichie, Troy, Stanmore, Holman, Holland, Schubert, Hall, Crocker, Purcell, Cowie.

ENGLAND:-
Ledgard, Danby, Ward, Ashcroft, Hilton, Cunliffe, Bradshaw, Gee, Egan, Gwyther, Phillips, Higgins, Street.

When play began it was quickly established that defences would dictate the outcome of the game and one slip up would prove to be costly. However, no one told the Australian players that fact or more likely their coach Vic Hey. The first half was almost all Australian attack after attack as they threw the ball around as if the ground was bone hard. The tourist defence in the main proved up to the task and it was twenty eights minutes before a point was scored. When the visitors strayed off side the referee McMahon penalized them and Churchill stepped up and placed the ball. He then scraped away a path through the mud for his run up and sent the ball over the cross bar and gave his team a 2-0 lead. It was a lead they were never to relinquish.

In truth the home side should have been further ahead as they were the better of the two sides. Purcell missed three penalties and then Ledgard pulled off a great tackle to stop Troy from scoring in the corner. The tourists had practically no chances to score as they seemed unable to cross the half way line. With the half coming to a close from a rare occasion they actually got close to the Australian try line. Ashcroft made a great break and when he was tackled the Australian centre McRichie barged into Bradshaw and flattened him. The referee gave the visitors a penalty much to the annoyance of the crowd. Ledgard stepped up and ignored the hooting and shouting of the crowd as they tried to put him off his kick. He sent it straight and true through the posts to level the scores at 2-2 as the half came to a close.

Both teams took to the field for the second half with clean jerseys but they did not stay that way for very long. The defensive battles intensified but again it was the home side that were playing the better. Schubert had won the first half scrums eight to six to assist his team in their attacks. In a turnup for the books McMahon had awarded the tourists more penalties than the home side. As the second half was underway the Englishmen suddenly began to look dangerous. Purcell had taken two shots at goal with no success and then in a rare attack Phillips went close to crossing for a three pointer after Bradshaw had worked the blind side of the scrum brilliantly. Having pulled the defence out he slipped the ball inside to Phillips who was held just short of the line.

A few minutes later in another attack Troy tackled his opposite number Danby without the ball and was penalized. Ward stepped up and the crowd held its breath as the kick flew through the air. As the ball sailed just wide of the posts a great roar went up and the crowd began to breath easy once more. With fifteen minutes gone in the second half the critical moment of the whole game arrived. It began when Purcell made a great run up the left-hand touchline. Incredibly the play the ball went back quickly and cleanly to the home side. Holman took the ball and immediately passed out to Stanmore, he in turn sent a quick pass on to McRichie. Driving straight McRichie then fed Middleton his centre partner the ball and he in turn timed his pass out to Roberts to perfection.

It was in truth a classic three-quarter line passing movement you would see in almost every game but given the conditions that afternoon the execution of the movement was faultless. Roberts had been given an overlap as the quickness of the passing had caught out the English defence. Ledgard was badly out of position and both Ashcroft and Ward had been pulled inside their opposite numbers. Roberts took the ball on what was probably the driest stretch of the ground and pinned back his ears. Hilton chased back and Roberts easily beat his despairing diving tackle to score in the corner.

The whole crowd erupted as did the home players almost all knew with that score the Ashes could well be on their way home after such a long time. Purcell missed the goal but with the score at 5-2 the visitors faced an uphill struggle. Try as they may the English could not get back into the game. In the dying seconds McMahon penalized the tourists for off side and Churchill simply tapped the ball into touch. The bell rang McMahon blew his whistle and the touch judge tucked the ball up his jumper there was no way he would give up that souvenir!

The crowd went absolutely crazy, programmes, hats newspapers were all thrown into the air. Hundreds of supporters climbed the fence and ran through ankle deep mud to get to the thirteen Aussie heroes. The players hugged each other and many were crying as they took delight in getting a thirty-year old monkey off their back. One man must have been extremely delighted and that man was coach Vic Hey after all his mid-week prediction that the six-foot three wingman Ron Roberts would win the game and the Ashes for his country had proved to be correct.

The players all swapped jerseys in the middle of the field before trooping off for a well-earned hot shower. Still the crowd would not depart the ground thousands gathered around the Members stand calling for the Australian skipper Churchill to come out to speak to them. Many stormed the stand and then tried to break into the Australian dressing room and police had to be summoned to break up the milling crowd such was the joy and excitement of the supporters at the historic win.

Harry Sunderland covered the game for the BBC and was faced with the almost impossible task of remaining impartial as he sent a dispatch over to England. As he wrote later:-

"As an Australian I naturally wanted the Kangaroos to win. I had been one of the selectors when we last won the Ashes in 1920- and I had been four times to England and seen our teams beaten by the narrowest of margins. After all these years, triumph had come at last."

The hero of the hour undoubtedly in the minds of supporters was the wingman Ron Roberts. He at the time did not realize just what he had been part of. In a superb interview by Tony Durkin for the Rugby League Week some thirty-six years after the event Roberts told him:-

"As soon as I had the ball in my hands, I knew I would score. There was no one between me and the try line and I was running on the only bit of firm ground on the field.

We all knew what an important match it was. They won the first Test in Sydney 6-4 but Australia came back to win 15-3 in Brisbane. July 22nd was Ashes Day.

At the time, the Ashes were the last thing on my mind. When I got the ball, all I thought about was scoring the try. After I scored all I thought about was winning the game. It wasn't until after the whistle that the impact of what had happened finally hit home.

The crowd poured onto the ground not as larrikins, but as Australian supporters with pride in their heart and there was a tear or two in the eyes of some pretty big tough muddy Australian players too."

(The try by Ron Roberts that won the Ashes for Australia)

There is no doubt that from a sporting point of view it was a momentous day for Australian sport in general and rugby league in particular. The Australians had waited thirty years to bring the Ashes home along with the Ashes Trophy donated by the City Tattersall's Club. Many in the game were of the opinion that they could now die happy knowing they had achieved what they had set out to do. (*The next two decades would see the two countries win and lose the Ashes with great regularity until the Australian domination that began in the 1960's only broken by the 1970 tourists took the trophy home for the very last time!*)

Unfortunately, George Oldroyd was in hot water yet again following the defeat. As he went to the English dressing-room he was followed by a reporter. On reaching the door he yet again promptly slammed it into the reporters face as he entered. Once inside he saw a reporter in the room speaking to the players, he immediately ordered him out. The players and Spedding spoke to him telling him it was alright but he was having none of it and insisted the reporter leave. The problem was that in Australia the reporters were always welcome to speak with players in the dressing-room following a game while in England they were not. It was once again an example of Oldroyds bombastic approach to problems

The English players were magnanimous in defeat feeling that the better team had won on the day. The skipper Ward felt that Vic Hey was the best Australian player along with Stanmore and Holman as he told Bill Corbett:-

"Hey was not on the field but his brains were out there and Stanmore and Holman used them to the utmost advantage."

Vice captain Joe Egan was equally gracious feeling that you could never win a game if your forwards were not on top and in the Test the Australian forwards had played superbly well.

Sadly George Oldroyd could not for the first time on the tour keep his opinions to himself telling Corbett:-

"The whole organization in Queensland needs reorganizing and then the game would go ahead there in leaps and bounds.

Nothing could be more efficient than the way the game is controlled in NSW where the officials are a credit to Rugby League.

Unfortunately, there is no comparison between the control in NSW and Queensland. The first thing the Queensland League should do is import the three best Sydney referees to coach their men.

Last Saturday in the Test we received as many penalties as we gave. In country matches in Queensland we were being penalized 30 and 40 times."

There is little doubt that he had a point but the time to raise it was before Council back in England on his return not following a Test which had seen the hosts win the Ashes for the first time in thirty years.

The players and officials with the Australian leg of the tour officially over prepared to leave Sydney. They were due to fly to New Zealand on the Sunday by flying boat a new experience for all I should have thought. Even then the weather had the final say as bad weather meant they were unable to leave on the Sunday and were forces to delay departure until 8.00am. on the Monday morning. In bright sunshine the tourists departed from Rose Bay in the flying boat bound for Auckland. Sadly, the depth of ill feeling Oldroyd had generated by his outbursts throughout the tour was such that only four officials from the rugby league authorities were there to see them off. In total there were only ten people there to see the tourists fly off at the tour's end. As the reporter for the Daily Telegraph wrote:-

"Australians yesterday gave the Englishmen a shabby farewell from Rose Bay flying base."

It was a fact that was not lost on people in the game back home who had been receiving reports of Oldroyds inappropriate outbursts as the tour progressed.

There were a number of interesting reports in the newspapers from the managers and some of the players. George Oldroyd reported that the Australian leg of the tour had generated record gate receipts and the tourists share came to £28,212 over £5,000 more than the 1946 tour. He told reporters that in his opinion the rain in Sydney had cost the tourists in the region of £10,000. The attendance at both Tests was considerably down due to the bad weather. He also revealed that the player bonus would be around £150 each in addition the player 'kitty' was around £200 made up of gifts, radio appearance fees and concert appearance fees. Oldroyd did reveal in the report some of the expenses the tourist faced while in the country. The travel costs by air and rail amounted to £2,300, accommodation for the party came to £2,200 while replacement playing kit came in at around £600. What he did not revel that he was more than anyone else responsible for the increase in flying costs!

Ken Gee who was on his second tour to the country was quite firm in his views when approached by reporters.

He was of the opinion that no matches should be played further north than Brisbane. He also had the view that the travel was far too demanding on players. He expressed the opinion others before him had made that it would be easier and more profitable to play Sydney club sides. The other interesting aside was made by a number of the players that perhaps five Tests should be played rather than just the three.

There was one very worrying issue not just for the managers but the game in general when it was revealed that the skipper Ernest Ward had been offered the post as none playing coach to Townsville up in Queensland. He expressed interest in the position and stated that he would discuss the matter with his wife once he got home. He did state that he would like his wife to see the country but she would make the decision as to whether he moved the family to Townsville. Ward was not the only player to receive offers as the Telegraph reporter reveal just prior to the players flying to New Zealand.

Doug Phillips and Tommy Bradshaw revealed they would consider returning but as migrants. The 1946 tourist Tommy McCue was at that time awaiting a passage to Australia for himself and his family and hoped to settle in Wollongong. Phillips and Bradshaw intended to discuss immigration with their wives on their return to England. The problem was a simple one if a player was offered a contract by an Australian club to travel down to play then that would not be allowed under the terms of the international transfer ban in place.

However, should a player decide to immigrate and settle in the country if he applied for clearance to return to the game the RFL had in past instances granted clearance. Both Phillips and Bradshaw were adamant that no club had made any offers to them. Phillips said that he had toured twice and just liked the place very much. It does seem there was a loop hole in the transfer ban if a player immigrated and then found a club, he could in fact begin playing again.

In the aftermath of this tremendously historic tour it is worth noting that first, a number of reporters had some sympathy with the visitors as they felt they had been badly treated by referees in Queensland in general and in the second Test in particular. Some felt that the display of refereeing had taken something of a shine of the series win. The other interesting thing is that that three-quarter line whose one concerted effort had won the Ashes for Australia, Roberts, Middleton, McRichie and Troy never pulled on a green and gold shirt again.

For the tourists however, it was for them a new country and a new tour this time in the land of the long white clouds.

CHAPTER SIX
(NZ two Tests lost a player home early)

There is no doubt that the tour party that landed in Auckland that day were a busted lot and a group that felt the weight of losing the Ashes for the first time in thirty years. In truth they had not really recovered from the debacle up in Queensland in the second Test never losing the feeling they had been robbed of victory by the referee. They now faced the prospect of putting together a patched-up team to face a very strong Kiwi team that had waited three year to gain revenge for a narrow two one series defeat in England. There was little doubt also that the majority of the players simply wanted to get on board a ship and sail home to their loved ones. Oldroyd and Spedding were not the managers to lift the spirits of their players that was for sure.

The problem was that awaiting them was a New Zealand outfit that was raring to go. They had waited three years to have another crack at the Englishmen following the tour to England. In that time many of the players who had toured were still playing the game and were now much more experienced. There was a feeling that they could beat the tourists and they were determined to have a good go at it. The two English managers on the other hand were juggling players, those that were fit, those carrying injuries and those who simply were unfit to play. Certainly, Horne would not pull on a jersey in the Dominion due to the Achilles tendon injury, Ashcroft was struggling also. In addition, there was still the belief that the managers were favouring certain players for Test matches rather than looking at form. It was a feeling that had been detected by reporters reasonably early on in the Australian leg of the tour.

The tourists arrived on the Monday and had to lift themselves for the first game which was to be played on Wednesday against Wellington down in Wellington at the Basin Reserve. They faced a trip down to the southern tip of North Island for the first encounter. After being officially welcomed by the League authorities the two managers had the task of selecting a team from the walking wounded. They eventually cobbled together a team which was:-

Ryan, Pollard, Cunliffe, Daniels, Danby, Williams, Bradshaw, Gwyther, Osmond, Featherstone, Phillips, Murphy, Traill.

On paper a very strong squad but many were carrying injuries and were tired after the long tour in Australia followed by the flight over. As it happened, they were far too strong for the opposition come out on top by a score of 40-15.

Once the game commenced the players faced the same difficulties from the local referee. While he was scrupulously fair to both sides his interpretation of the rules was different once again from that in Australia. The tourists were on the wrong side of a penalty count mainly for scrum and play the ball offences. It was an old familiar story.

Before the game Oldroyd was once more courting controversy when he spoke with a reporter for the Auckland paper when he arrived. He told the reporter:-

"Arrangements in Queensland were rotten. He highly praised the treatment the team had received in New South Wales and New Zealand."

It was obvious that such a remark was going to make its way back to Australia and so it did. The Wide Bay rugby league authorities were furious and demanded that the Queensland authorities take action. They pointed out when the players were in Wide Bay the football manager Spedding had declared freely that the team had been given an excellent reception. Once again, the two managers were not singing from the same hymn sheet. The comment also upset reporter Harry Sunderland greatly as we shall see later.

That game over the tourists continued on their travels this time to Christchurch down on South Island. This time awaiting them was a very strong and determined International side. The visitors already had one unwanted record, that of losing the Ashes they did not want another that of losing three Test matches in a row. In the buildup to the game it appeared that George Oldroyd could once more not refrain from entering into a local controversy.

The game was scheduled to be played at the Show Grounds in Christchurch while the authorities would have liked to have used Victory Park. It was the age-old story of the tremendous influence the rugby union authorities held in New Zealand. It was they who covertly had applied pressure to the Victory Park Board to withhold permission because as the winter tenants of the ground they had the power of veto. Oldroyd issued a challenge via the newspapers for the Board to meet with him to discuss the possibility of the ground being used for future big rugby league games.

The Press reported that Oldroyd said :-

"I would be prepared to come back from Greymouth, from Auckland, in fact I would even be prepared to stay after my ship sails if I thought it would do any good and help future touring teams to be allowed to use the best grounds wherever they play."

He went on to say at the reception held for the players following the game in Wellington:-

"In England the Rugby Union and League co-operate with each other when either association is playing big matches and during the war the two combined to raise £10,000 as a benefit for the Royal Air Force, and they played on our grounds. There was no distinction there. Since then we have fought a war against hatred yet it still exists. It is a poor compensation for our fighting men."

The sentiments expressed may well have been true but it would seem to many that he was only adding fuel to the fire. The Victoria Ground had been denied to tour parties from the 1920 onward. When the 1946 tourists had arrived and been denied the use of the ground there had been massive protests from local folks. The argument being that both countries had fought side by side in World War 2. Sadly, the union authorities were unmoved and refused permission. It was a New Zealand problem and one Oldroyd should have left to the home League authorities to sort out. At that reception Oldroyd expressed the opinion that the final Test in Sydney should really not have been played due to the condition of the ground. Again, he was probably correct with that statement but had it not been played there was no time in the schedule to rearrange the game. The point was not lost on some that had the game not gone ahead with each country winning one game the Ashes would have been retained by England!

With the tourists in Christchurch at last the weather relented and clear blue skies were seen for the first time in many days. On the Saturday at the Show Ground over 10,000 paid to witness the game. The pitch was in almost ideal condition there was just the odd greasy patch. Both teams relished the opportunity to actually play the game on a dry surface. The two teams for this first Test were:-

NEW ZEALAND
White, Forrest, Baxter, Hough, Robertson, Barchard, Haig, Hardwick, Hurndell, McBride, Newton, Davidson, Johnson.

ENGLAND
Ledgard, Pollard, Ward, Ashcroft, Hilton, Williams, Pepperell, Gee, Egan, Featherstone, Higgins, Ryan, Traill.

It is interesting to note that even at this period in the game's history in the country the journalists still listed players in the rugby union style. They listed the three quarters as Pollard, Ward and Hilton while Ashcroft was referred to as 'the second five-eight! The managers had rung the changes most notably Pepperell got the scrum half berth over Bradshaw while Martin Ryan had been left out and Ledgard was in at full back. Featherstone who was now really hitting top form consistently was preferred to Gwyther and Traill was to play rather than Street.

Ward won the toss and it was the home side who kicked off into the sun to get the game started. England went on the attack almost at once but were penalized for off side. White stepped up and with just a minute or so gone converted the penalty and the Kiwis were in the lead 2-0. As the game progressed the tourists tried to attack at almost every opportunity. They were met by strong defence and were guilty of handling errors at the wrong time. Slowly the Englishmen got to the pace of the game and began to put together some good attacking moves when forwards and backs combined.

Gee leading from the front strode though the home defence and put Williams into the clear. With a try looking a certainty unfortunately Williams slipped on the greasy turf and the chance was lost. At this point both sides were playing good football both in attack and defence. Chances were going begging at both ends of the field but it was the home side that struck for the first try. It came from a mistake by the normally so safe Ledgard who misfielded a high kick. The home players quick to follow up kicked the ball on and quick hands saw Hardwick run around behind the posts for the first try of the game. White added the extras and the home side were leading 7-0.

The score spurred on the visitors who attacked with even greater frequency but could not make the vital break through. With play on the twenty-five yard line of the Englishmen they were penalized once again for off side. White once again punished then and took the score to 9-0. The game was seemingly slipping away from the tourists. Gee was again in the thick of the action at both ends of the field. He saved a certain try by kicking the ball out of the hands of Robinson as he chased a kick through over the try line. A few minutes later at the other end of the field as he had done before Gee took the ball through the defensive line. His pass in field to the ever-supporting Williams set him free and a forty-yard arcing run saw him out pace White to score under the posts. Skipper Ward made no mistake and from seeming out of it they were back in the contest at 9-5.

With the first half coming to a close the tourists struck once again. Traill collected the ball and timed his pass to

Ward perfectly. Ward in turn showed all his craft and guile to send Pollard flying through a gap to score again under the posts. As Ward's conversion sailed though the posts the referee blew his whistle for half time. As the players went into the dressing rooms the Englishmen in truth against the run of play were in the lead 9-10. The feeling was that the home side would not come back from that set back in the second half.

The defence of the Kiwis may have wilted a little as the first half was coming to an end but it was back at its high standard as the second half began. It needed to be as England continued to attack from all parts of the field. The homesters were also throwing the ball about as well. With play on the visitors twenty-five Traill strayed off side and White gladly accepted the two points to give his side the lead again at 11-10. It was then that the game was turned on its head.

There was only six minutes gone in the half when Ledgard went into a scrummage with the ball and when play broke down, he was still on the ground. It quickly became apparent that the injury was serious and a stretcher was summoned. Ledgard was taken from the field by the ambulance men and Ward was forced to shuffle the team. He went to full back and then moved Williams into the centre. The second row Higgins was pulled out of the pack to play at stand-off. With hindsight pulling Higgins out of the pack was not the best call. Up to that time Egan had been shading the scrums but now in a depleted scrum he was unable to win enough ball for his team.

Starved of the ball and faced with determined tackling the visitors attack began to struggle a bit. On the occasions they actually put together good attacking plays they were invariably penalized for one offence or another. The five English forwards strived mightily and lifted the crowd on numerous occasions as did the home side with their heroic defending. As the game went on it became more apparent that the loss of Ledgard was becoming more obvious and it was inevitable that something had to give. Sadly, it was the visitors at a scrum on their own ten-yard line. The New Zealand pack won yet another scrum and Barchard with a clever change of direction fooled the defence to score in the corner. White stepped up and hammered the final nail in the visitor's coffin when he landed a superb pressure goal from the touch line to make the final score 16-10 to the home side.

When the final whistle went the crowd rose to both sides after what had been a classic Test match. For the Englishmen once again, it was a case of what might have been. Had Ledgard not been injured, had they not had to play over half an hour with only twelve men then it could well have been a different story. The reality was that they had now lost three Test matches in a row and there were still more matches to play. As ever Ward the skipper was magnanimous in defeat praising the Kiwi players and making no reference to Ledgard's loss. As was ever the case there was little time to dwell on the defeat as the next game was to be played on the other side of South Island at Graymouth.

The game was to be played on Wednesday the 30th July at Wingham Park and the opposition were West Coast. As they left Christchurch, they left Ledgard behind in hospital his injured back still being assessed by the doctors. The game on the coast turned out to be a little more difficult than expected the home side going down 21-15. There is little doubt that the players were fast approaching the last remaining stamina and energy they possessed and this with still one more Test match on the schedule. The play of the tourists was sluggish and labored. The referee once again saw little right in the way they scrummaged or played the ball and the resulting penalties continually slowed down play. Joe Egan came in for a little criticism for his lackluster performance particularly in the loose.

It was only to be expected I suppose when you look at the three-quarter line for the visitors in that game, Pollard, Cunliffe, Danby and Ratcliffe. While great players in their own right they had not played together on the tour so obviously lacked cohesion. The one good thing to emerge from the game was that there were no injuries to the players. With the game over and the hospitality and reception at an end the players were able to travel back to Auckland where they would remain for the final three games of the tour.

On the Saturday the opposition were Auckland and in an effort to rest tired players the two managers once again rejigged the team that was to play. While the game was won by a score of 26-17 the score line did not reflect the domination of the tourists. Williams the stand-off dominated the whole game with his attacking brilliance. He was closely followed by Street who seemed to be everywhere as was the old war horse Ken Gee. It was however, a tired display once again and most players simply did just what was necessary to win the game and no more.

As the players were preparing for the last of the mid-week matches there was more upset for the players. The jinx that had affected the wingmen in the tour party all through the tour raised its ugly head once again. News came via a telegram to the managers to say that one of Arthur Daniels family and been taken seriously ill. That being the case he was required to return home as quickly as possible. There was no way he could sail with the party and arrive back in England in around five weeks. Arrangements were quickly made for the player to fly home. So, it was that on the 8th August the players said their farewells to Daniels as he departed for the airport and home. He joined the prop Naughton who was on the high seas at that time also returning from the tour early with a broken leg.

While the managers would have liked to rest players the injury list would not allow it. Key players like Ashcroft and Horne were missing and unlikely to be right for the final Test. Hilton and Ratcliffe were not showing the sort of form that had gained them selection for the tour in the first place. Dandy was the bright light in all the darkness but he was being utilized more as a wing than a centre. Ledgard while not seriously injured following the Test defeat had not recovered sufficiently to come into contention for selection either for the mid-week game or the Test match. It was a juggling act once more the managers faced if they were to put out a side capable of beating the Kiwis who now had their tails up.

With the final mid-week game to be played at Huntly to the south of Auckland the players not required remained in their headquarters. The game itself proved to be of little consequence for the tourists as they won by a runaway score of 51-5. The interesting thing about the match was that either by design or plain good luck the visitors only kicked the ball away twice in the whole game. When even the opposition kicked to Cunliffe at full back he ran the ball back to his team mates in the style of Martin Ryan. With the score at 22-2 at half time the game was effectively over and the tourists simply threw the ball about at will. With Bradshaw and Pepperell as half backs and constantly switching between scrum half and stand off the opposition were totally mesmerized by their slight of hand and tricks.

The game over it was back to Auckland to prepare for the final game against New Zealand. As game day arrived the poor weather relented somewhat and the Saturday turned out to be ideal for playing the game. The home side as expected with no injury problems named an unchanged side to oppose the tourists. The managers of the Englishmen on the other hand did not have such luxury. Ashcroft was still unfit to play which created a massive hole in the three-quarter line. With Ledgard out Cunliffe was called upon to fill in at full back. Ratcliffe was also struggling and so Danby was put out on the wing instead of in the centre. As on other occasions Street was deputed to leave the pack to occupy the vacant centre position. In the half backs they two managers not for the first time opted for tried and tested and Williams partnered Bradshaw now seemingly back in favour. The pack more or less picked itself.

The teams for this final Test were:-

NEW ZEALAND
White, Forrest, Baxter, Hough, Robertson, Barchard, Haig, Hardwick, Hurndell, McBride, Newton, Davidson, Johnson.

ENGLAND
Cunliffe, Danby, Ward, Street, Hilton, Williams, Bradshaw, Featherstone, Egan. Gee, Ryan, Higgins, Traill.

When the game kicked off at Carlaw Park, which proved to be totally inadequate for the numbers wishing to see the game. For an hour before the kick-off the turn stiles were closed as the ground capacity had been reached leaving vast numbers of supporters milling around outside the ground. The game followed the same pattern as the first Test with the English backs being superior but the home defence being up to the task. Williams played exceptionally well but he and Bradshaw were kept on a tight rein by the home side.

In the opening encounters it was the black shirts that seemed to be endlessly attacking and with ten minutes gone all they had to show was a White penalty to lead 2-0. This sparked the visitors into greater efforts and first Williams and then Featherstone launched attacks but could not convert them into a score. Finally, it was Williams who cracked the home defence and fed the ball out to the centre Street. He in turn continued driving for the try line and when about to be tackled passed on to Ward who put the ball over the whitewash. Unfortunately, he could not convert his own try but the tourists were in the lead 2-3.

That lead was extended when the usually reliable White at full back mis-handled a high kick. His mistake was capitalized on by the second row Ryan who simply tapped the ball ahead, picked up and scored. With Ward adding the extras the lead was stretched out to 2-8. A few minutes later following a number of penalties against the visitors White once again secured two points to close the score to 4-8. There was little doubt the visitor's backs were superior when they had the ball in hand but the home defence stood firm. Then a little against the run of play Baxter and Hough combined to beat Danby and Hough went in for a try wide out that

While could not convert. The score line however had closed to 7-8.

Within a minute of the restart the home side were in once more. Haig from a scrum fed the ball to McBride who passed on to Hurndell who when clear immediately passed back to Haig. He simply bumped off the attempted tackle by Ward and score another unconverted try. From seemingly in control of the game the visitors went in for the half time break actually behind 10-8. In the break the English felt all they had to do was continue to throw the ball about and the scores would come.

The Kiwis perhaps sensing they had been lucky to score two tries realized that it was their defence that would win the game. As the second half commenced, they simply played everything as tight as they could. They moved quickly up on the opposition giving them little room for maneuver and when they had the ball kept it amongst the forwards. The tourists switched Street to the wing and brought into the centre Danby and simply sought to attack from anywhere on the field. As the game became a bit of an arm wrestle it inevitably led to incidents of fists and boots flying and the referee was called on a number of times to issue cautions to players from both sides.

Ironically midway through the half the same situation as had occurred for the visitors in the first Test reoccurred. Street now out on the wing damaged an ankle and was taken from the field for treatment. Higgins was withdrawn from the pack to replace him and it was while down to twelve men the Kiwis struck a mortal blow. Haig not for the first time broke clear from a scrum and fed McBride who carried the break on. The whole Kiwi three-quarter line handled before Robertson crossed for the three points. Haig who had started the move stepped up and slotted over the extra two to take the lead out to 15-8.

When the game restarted the injured Street returned to the fray but the damage had been done. The visitors again launch attack after attack but the home side defence once more stood firm. Then as is always the case it was the under pressure Kiwis that struck and it was Haig who was the architect. He launched an attack and followed up as Robertson and Forrest continued for the try line. Forrest threw a pass inside and Haig shot over for a well- deserved try. This time it was Davidson who added the extras and at 20-8 the game was now out of reach for the Englishmen.

With the game coming to a close it was Danby who was injured and helped from the field. The twelve men however, struck when Williams broke through and fed Cunliffe in support. When tackled Cunliffe passed out to Featherstone and from forty yards out the prop showed all a clean pair of heels to score under the posts and Ward converted to make the score 20-13. Danby returned to the field and with the momentum swinging back towards the tourists once more, once again circumstances conspired against them.

Throughout the second half whenever the ball had been kicked into the crowd the officials had great difficulty getting the spectators to return it. Of the four balls in use as play was coming to an end only one was available the other three were up various jumpers of the supporters. When the last ball was hoofed into the crowd it mysteriously disappeared. The game was held up for several minutes while another ball was found to allow the game to continue. By the time it made an appearance all the momentum generated by the visitors had been dissipated.

If that were not bad enough just as the game was coming to a close and with the Kiwis on the attack the crowd unable to contain their excitement invaded the pitch. Hardwick with ball in hand charged for the line and looked sure to score until he was felled by a stray schoolboy who he sent sprawling and the try was lost. With pandemonium seemingly, the norm the whistle went for full time. The tourists had lost an unprecedented fourth consecutive Test match a record none of them relished.

Interestingly in his match report Harry Sunderland publicized a fact that had been buzzing around the reporters for quite a while. As was mentioned earlier there was an anger amongst some players that the tour party was looked upon by the managers as being in truth two parties. One was the so called 'Test' outfit the other was referred to by Sunderland as 'the Sunday school treats'. Sunderland wrote:-

"Most critics now agree that the form of the present tourists in big matches as distinct from the 'Sunday school treats' against country teams, has not been up to the standard of teams lead by Wagstaffe, Sullivan and Parkin."

What Sunderland did was write what most other reporters knew but Spedding and Oldroyd always denied was the case. It was certainly not the first time that such claims had been made with regard to touring teams and sadly on future tour it seemed to become the norm as the mid-week teams became known as the 'ham and eggers."

With the game completed and all the formalities wrapped up there was little time left for sightseeing. On the Monday the tourists went aboard the Tamora and set sail for home officially the playing side of the tour at an end. The recriminations of the tour particularly the Australian leg were though far from over. The two managers were well aware that questions would be asked of their management particularly as the Ashes were now in the hands of the Australians. The other issue that reporters had suppressed to a large extend on the tour was the perceived differences between the two managers.

Through out the tour in Australia Tom Spedding the player manager had steadfastly remained silent when questioned about the refereeing controversies particularly in Queensland. George Oldroyd the business manager on the other hand had been quick to vent his fury at the officials and comment on matters that really were not his concern. These matters would need to be dealt with in the tour report that they would present to Council on their return. It would have been a difficult sea trip for the two as they wrestled with the problems they had faced and how they were to present them to the Rugby League Board once they arrived home.

CHAPTER SEVEN
(Home to face the music – whitewash claims)

When the tourists returned home the players as always returned to their own clubs and awaited news from the Rugby League Council. Once the two managers reported back to Council with regard to both the financial situation of the tour along with any disciplinary issues encountered then the players would know just what their share of the profits would be. The managers would have prepared the report and hopefully been ready to deliver it to the Council at the beginning of October.

Given the controversies that the tour had thrown up reporters were keen to speak to the managers. As had been the case in Australia Spedding preferred to keep his own council. He told reporters:-

"Trouble, what trouble. There was a little bother about Australian interpretation of the rules that's all."

Oldroyd on the other hand was quick to vent his fury to any prepared to listen:-

"I shall leave no stone unturned so that future teams to Australia shall not suffer the disappointments we had on our recent trip.

The English Rugby League Council must hear my comments first. I shall have plenty to say in the right place at the right time. But believe me I shall be frank."

When his comments got back to the Australian Board Chairman Harry Flegg was furious and replied to the comments:-

"I am surprised at the statements by Mr. Oldroyd. When he talks of the right time, I hope he will talk of the way he acted on the tour. If Mr. Oldroyd had acted in the same manner as Mr. Spedding everybody would have been happy."

On the 4th October the Rugby League staged the tour ending friendly when the tourists played the rest in a game. On this occasion the tourists won the match 23-16. However, the tourist's felt the brunt of the supporters, anger at what had occurred down under. They booed freely every time the tourists handled the ball. The touring players did win the game easily.

That done the Council was ready to hear just what the two managers had to say. Unfortunately, we have little idea just what went on as strange as it seems the report written by the managers is not in the minutes of that period. Also, the meeting discussing the report was held in camera. That being the case we must inevitably rely on newspaper reports for any information they may have gleaned. What we do know is that such were the issues raised by and against the managers that the Council felt that further time was needed to consider the report and so decided to discuss the matter further at a meeting toward the end of the month. The meeting was held on 30th October.

The meetings to discuss the tour were held in camera so all news was really suppressed which seems to be the norm in this game of ours. The Secretary Bill Fallowfield then released news to the reporters but only that news he felt acceptable. The Daily Telegraph in Sydney on the 1st November 1950 carried a report. Under the headline:-

ENGLAND ACCEPTS CRITICISM OF TOUR

It seems the Rugby League accepted the criticism made by the manager George Oldroyd with regard to the very poor standard of refereeing. The two games drawing the ire of Oldroyd were the match against Queensland and more importantly the second Test in Brisbane. The managers also voiced their complaints about the standard of accommodation the players were allocated while up in Townsville. While the meeting was held in camera George Oldroyd did himself no favour's by speaking to the reporters following that October 30th meeting:-

"The League asked many questions about the tour. It also discussed complaints from Queensland League and a letter which criticized me. The letter charged me with not having attended some games and having missed some functions. However, the meeting accepted the manager's report."

You cannot help but feel that Oldroyd was in the words of Shakespeare "protesting too much." What he does reveal is that such was the ill feeling he and he alone generated in Queensland that the Queensland League felt compelled to write to The Rugby League with regard to his behavior. In that report sent to Council the Queensland Board enclosed clippings from the newspapers containing the statements Oldroyd had made to support their complaints.

The following day Eddie Waring writing again for the Daily Telegraph in Sydney wrote aa article outlining the recommendations the Council felt should be implemented for future tours. It is worth reading in its entirety:-

"The English Rugby League will make recommendations to the Australian Board of Control for future tours.
It decided this last night after having discussed the managers' report of its team's recent tour of Australia.
The recommendations are:-
The best referee in Australia should be chosen for Tests irrespective of his state.
The Board of Control be the only body empowered to discipline English players ordered from the field.
(The Australian Board of Control's policy is to restrict the appointment of a Test referee to the state in which the Test is being played.)
During the recent tour the Board refused a request from the English managers messers George Oldroyd and Tom Spedding to make New South Wales referees eligible for the second Test in Brisbane.

Also during the tour the Englishmen were annoyed at the suspension of half-back Tommy Bradshaw and prop forward Elwen Gwyther for one match. (Queensland officials suspended Bradshaw and Ipswich officials Gwyther.)

During the discussion the English League bombarded the managers with questions on the tour.

It also heard allegations from Queensland about the managers.

Mr. R.F. Anderson who had been co-manager of the 1932 and 1936 English touring teams asked Mr Oldroyd if he had not been indiscrete in certain remarks he had made on tour.

He also questioned Mr. Oldroyd about the announcement of teams in Australia.

The managers denied a suggestion that there had been trouble between them."

The suggestion made here by Waring is simply confirmation of rumours that had followed the tour party throughout the Australian leg of the tour. The reporters in Australia hinted of difficulties between the two managers and certainly if you examine the controversial comments made on the tour, they come from Oldroyd. In fact, Tom Spedding the team manager seems to have said very little to the press while on tour. There was also the belief even amongst the players that the managers had formed a Test thirteen and a mid-week thirteen very early on the tour. Some players felt that it mattered not how well they played they would not be selected for the big games.

The contrast between the two managers could not really have been greater. Oldroyd was from the Dewsbury club and steeped in the game. On the other-hand Tom Spedding was the Master of Ceremonies for the Belle Vue Entertainment complex in Manchester yet he had been given the role of team manager while Oldroyd was the business manager. Given the rumours that abounded the British press did little for whatever reasons. It could well have been they did not wish to upset the authorities after all their bread and butter depended on a good relationship with club officials and players. Also, back then there was a tendency amongst reporters not to publish stories that were detrimental to the game. Whatever the reasons we can find little criticism in English newspapers.

It was left to the Australian Harry Sunderland writing in the Sunday Sun on the 5th of November in response to the Council's backing of the two managers. In truth they could have done nothing else after all they had appointed them. They were never going to criticize the two of them publicly what was said in private is another matter. Sunderland's article is worth looking at in its entirety:-

"No balance sheet on the finances of the English Rugby League team's tour of Australia this year has been presented. English League Secretary Bill Fallowfield told me that this week but he said he

hoped to do so shortly. I have learned that the Rugby League Council is dealing with the whole matter with caution.

Though the team has been home several weeks business manager George Oldroyd's books weren't handed to Fallowfield until October 25th five days before the Council met.

Beside the two managers' report and those from the Australian Board of Control and Queensland League the English Council had a letter from me.

I described how the tourists had been entertained in Queensland and received record gates-much bigger on a population basis than they did in NSW. My letter stated, in view of these facts, how disappointed I was at Oldroyd's attack on Queensland.

I pointed out that he had failed to attend some matches and had flown thousands of miles, while his co-manager Spedding and the team had travelled everywhere by train."

It would have not been viewed well by Council that Oldroyd have travelled separately from the rest on a good number of occasions. They would have been equally scathing of the delay in presenting the financial report to Council. Such matters were always of the highest importance. Just why they treated the matter with caution still remains a mystery to this day. It is difficult to understand why there was a delay in presenting the balance sheet. Equally problematical was why the Council were treating it with such caution. When the report was finalized the Rugby League profit was £10,350 a record so why the delay.

What is also puzzling is just why Oldroyd did so much travelling by air and why he was not in attendance at some matches. In another article Sunderland listed the games Oldroyd had missed, Cootamundra, Kempsey, Forbes, Toowoomba, the Brisbane League game and the game at Gunnedah. Six games out of nineteen did not sit well with Council members. It was such actions which would have only added to the growing disunity within the tour party. Players were spending many hours on trains travelling huge distances to games while one of the managers was flying to and from games and missing others. This was an issue Oldroyd did not address in public.

In his defence regarding his statements to the Australian press and at functions Oldroyd claimed he had been mis-quoted by reporters who were out to embarrass him. The Council did have copies of the articles but still in public backed their manager, in truth they had little other option. There is little doubt also that Oldroyd was the dominant managerial figure throughout the tour even speaking to the press on matters of team selection which in truth was the domain of Spedding. All in all, it was a very unsatisfactory situation and one Council was evidently unhappy about.

Their pigeons had come home to roost for Council for it was they who had selected these two opposing managerial styles. Surely, they would have been well aware of Oldroyd's management style and how it would not sit well with the Australians. Perhaps there was an element of complacency feeling that there was little or no chance the Ashes would be lost.

The players would have been delighted at that news of such a huge profit from the tour for they were to share 40% of the tour profits and that came to £160 per player also a record and around £36 more that the 1946 tourists had earned. With the tour over and reports in the Council would have mulled over the tour that is for sure. The Ashes had been lost for the first time in thirty years and yet the players selected were the best available. It would have been easy to blame the loss on poor refereeing in the second Test but there were other factors at play. There is little doubt that the two managers had not worked well together during the tour also Oldroyd had over stepped the mark on a number of occasions embarrassing the home union.

The Australians had complained that the announcement of the touring team to play had often been late in its delivery to both the home authorities and the local reporters. Once again, a great discourtesy which had not gone down well either in Australia or at home. An even greater discourtesy must surely have been the refusal to support a farewell tour dinner by the NSW Rugby League something that had occurred at the end of every other tour. Council would have viewed such action by the managers in a bad light.

Despite of all these factors the one important thing is that the Ashes had been lost, and lost for the first time in a long time. What was important was to analyse just why that had occurred, were the players simply not good enough. One thing was certain the style of play in this country had changed, gone was the dependence on tight forward rucking in favour of a fast, flowing type of football. It was a style similar to that of the Australians which perhaps worked against the tourists on the tour.

Certainly, the first and third Test matches were played in the most appalling conditions and could have gone either way. As it was one went to the home side the other to the visitors. The second Test in Brisbane all agreed was dominated by refereeing decisions and the dismissal of two English players which changed the game. I would also argue the managers or more specific one in particular contributed to the loss of the Ashes. There is no doubt the tour party became fractured and players felt their efforts counted for very little when it came to selection for the big games. This was an attitude that neither manager seemed capable of dispelling. We can of course speculate forever on what went wrong but the bottom line is the Ashes were now in the hands of the Australians.

I suppose the last word on this tour that signaled the End of an Era should be seen when the 1954 tour was being selected. In a break from what had been a long established protocol on all other tours where one manager from the previous visit was appointed to return.

In 1954 neither Oldroyd or Spedding were selected for either manager's position for that tour. In addition when the selection committee to select the touring party was set up Oldroyd was not voted on! When the Australians visited this country in 1952 the Ashes were won back in a two to one series victory. That however is another story.

PEN PICTURES

It is important to inform the reader that the pen pictures contained here are written by the author. They are intended to give a brief picture of the player and his playing career leading up to the time of being selected for the tour back in 1950.

EARNEST WARD Bradford Northern (Captain)

Ward is making his second visit to Australia and New Zealand this time as captain of the team. Born in Dewsbury he joined the Bradford club in 1941. Since that time, he has won every honour the game has to offer. Still considered to be one of the most skillful centres in the game today. He is also a goal kicker of some renown and can be relied upon to score a handful of goals on this tour. He and his vice-captain hooker Egan take a wealth of rugby experience with them on this tour.

JOE EGAN Wigan (Vice-Captain)

The vice-captain is still considered to be one of the best hookers in the English game although there are some in the game who questioned his selection. His ability to win the ball in the scrum coupled with his outstanding play in the ruck and loose play will be invaluable on the hard Australian grounds. He is another making his second trip down under and he like Ward has won every honour the game has to offer. In partnership with his Wigan prop colleague Gee they will provide formidable opposition to Australian sides.

FULL BACKS

MARTIN RYAN Wigan

The 27 year old joined his home town club of Wigan in 1940 and early on filled the centre role. Since switching to full back he has been a revelation redefining the way full backs play the game. Not for him the kicking duels rather he quickly runs the ball back up to his players to launch an attack. Even though he his making a second trip down under he will be new to players in Australia as on his last visit a Hernia injury curtailed his tour to just four games. His attacking style of play will cause all sorts of problems for the opposition.

JIM LEDGARD Leigh

The 28 year old was born in Wakefield but came into the game first with the Dewsbury club back in 1943. He won an England cap with that club along with Great British honours. In 1948 the Leigh club paid a record £2,650 fee for his services. He is a goal kicker of great skill and his positional play and kicking from hand has seen him win many a kicking dual. He is a contrast to the new style of full back play seen by his colleague Ryan. He will not be one to let the tour party down whenever he takes to the field.

WINGERS

ARTHUR DANIELS Halifax

Daniels is a Welshman who hails from Pontyberem who joined the Halifax club in 1945 at the end of the conflict. It was only in the 1948-49 season that he gained a permanent spot in the Yorkshire outfits first team. He quickly showed just what he was capable of when he won representative honours for his native Wales in the League code. He went on to have a strong Test series against the Australian tourists on their recent visit to this country. His strong running style will be admirably suited to the fast hard grounds he will meet in Australia.

JACK HILTON Wigan

Hilton began his career with the Salford club and on one occasion scored six tries for that club in a game against Leigh. In 1942 he joined his home town club of Wigan and went on to win representative honours while at the club. He impressed the selectors in the England Wales trial game back in March with his speed and also his defence both qualities that are needed on the tour. Hilton who was somewhat of a controversial selection in certain quarters has speed to burn and there is no doubt he will be pushing for a Test place against stiff opposition from his own tour team mates.

GORDEN RATCLIFFE Wigan

Yet another player from the Wigan club who while originally not selected was included when Williams declined to tour. He joined Wigan in 1945 and has won representative honours while at the club. He is considered to be one of the fastest wingmen in the game today and has put that speed to good effect as can be seen by his try scoring ability. He and Hilton his club mate will give the tourists great finishing power when they play the Australian teams. He is equally at home on either wing and this versatility is very important when the team is on the other side of the world. He like Hilton will be pushing hard for a place in the Test team.

ROY POLLARD Dewsbury

Pollard is just making his way in the game with the Yorkshire outfit. He comes from excellent rugby league stock however being the son of Charles Pollard who toured Australia and New Zealand. His uncle Earnest Pollard also made the visit down under as well. The twenty three year old joined the Dewsbury club in 1949 and his form this season was such that the selectors felt they could not leave him out of the tour party. He has already represented England at international level. This has been achieved after only a short time in the professional ranks. Yet another strong running and strong tackling wingman who should be a force on the firmer Australian grounds.

CENTRES

ERNEST ASHCROFT Wigan

This experienced centre joined his home town club in 1942 as a seventeen year old. While only twenty-five he has won every honour the game has to offer. He is considered to be one of the craftiest centres in the game today. Having met the Australians on home soil he will be looking forward to jousting with them once again in their backyard. He and Hilton form a very dangerous attacking weapon for the Wigan club and it is hoped they will produce that form on this tour. He is a player the Australians will fear when they face him.

JACK CUNLIFFE Wigan

Cunliffe seems to have been around for ever but his form this season has been outstanding. He joined his home town outfit back in 1939 and it seems he is equally at home wherever he plays in the backs. A talented ball player, goal kicker and reader of the game. It is this versatility which is much needed on a tour that made him one of the first names the selectors added to the team sheet. Given he can play in any position he will be pushing for a Test position anywhere from full back to stand-off. He is a strong running and hard defending player the Australians fear playing against.

TOM DANBY Salford

Although a product of County Durham Danby signed for the Salford club from the Harlequins rugby union club in 1949. He had already been capped by England at rugby union before switching codes. His form in this his first season in the new code has been outstanding and while his selection may well have shocked many the selectors felt he could not be left out. He is equally at home in the centre or on the wing and again it is this versatility that adds strength to his claim for selection. He is a hard, strong running player who has a deceptive change of pace and a neat sidestep. His style of play will be new to the Australians and it is thought he will prove to be one of the new young stars on the tour.

STAND-OFF

WILLIE HORNE Barrow

The twenty-eight year old first played for the Oldham club but declined their offer of a contract to sign for his home town club Barrow in 1943. He was just twenty-one at the time but quickly became a prolific points scorer for the club. It was his ability to set his three-quarters on the attack that caused the selectors to include him in the team. He is no stranger to Australia having made the trip back in 1946 when the Ashes were retained. The opposition down under will be fully aware of his skill and know how. The selectors feel that if he remains fit and healthy, he will prove to be a thorn in the side of Australian teams.

DICKIE WILLIAMS Leeds

Williams is another Welshman in the party hailing from Mountain Ash in the Principality. He played for that club before moving to the Bristol rugby union outfit before being spotted and brought to Leeds in 1944. Since switching codes, he has won representative honours with Wales and now finds himself in the tour party. Williams has phenomenal acceleration from a standing start and an elusive body swerve. While somewhat of an individualist in his style of play the selectors feel this will suit the more experienced three-quarters in the party. They will be better able to read his play and capitalize on the breaks he will make in attack. The firm grounds and open style of play of Australia are it is felt tailor made for Williams.

SCRUM HALF

TOMMY BRADSHAW Wigan

Another of the Wigan contingent in the tour party Bradshaw is considered by many to be the finest scrum half in the game today. Now thirty he has lost none of his attacking flair and ability to lead his team around the field. He reads a game very well and knows when to play the game tight and when to open play up. He is another who has won every honour the game has to offer. The selectors feel that Bradshaw will more than uphold the tradition of touring side scrum halves and will match the likes of Parkin when he gets down to Sydney. He will relish feeding the scrum to his Wigan team mates Gee and Egan.

ALBERT PEPPERELL Workington Town

Pepperell is a somewhat controversial selection in the eyes of many but not those of the selectors. He is one of three brothers playing the game today and has by his displays for the Workington club this season fully justified his selection. He is a strong running and tackling scrum half who has the ability to release his three-quarters at the right time. He also seems never to be too far from the ball when it is in play be it on attack or defending his own line. It was his play for his native Cumberland against the Australian tourists back in 1948 when he led his team to a 5-4 victory that first brought him to the notice of the selectors. New to the Australians he may well provide them with more than a few headaches.

PROP FORWARDS

KEN GEE Wigan

The thirty four year old Wigan prop has been the mainstay of the English pack for many a year. Making his second tour to Australia the green and gold will be fully aware of what is coming to face them. Gee has won ever honour in the game. Since joining his home town club as a nineteen year old he has made the prop position his own. His partnership with his team mate Egan is considered to be one of the best ball winning combinations in the game at the present time. There is no doubt the younger players in the party will be pushing him for that Test place but they will face the stiffest of opposition. This season he has added another string to his bow namely that as a goal kicker having scored well over a hundred goals for his club.

JIM FEATHERSTONE Warrington

Featherstone first joined the Wigan club before transferring his allegiance to Warrington after the war ended. His form this season has been such that many considered him to be the best all round prop forward in our game. A big strong forward who is deceptively quick over the ground in the loose play makes him equally valuable both in the scrums and also loose play. With him and Gee on either side of a hooker it will ensure a more than equal supply of the ball from the scrum down under. He is the modern style of mobile forward that will be needed on the firm Australian grounds.

FRED HIGGINS Widnes

On past tours the Widnes club has provided a number of great prop forwards and Higgins is no exception. His two elder brothers Jack and Alec are also professional players so he is from good stock. A strong running player who is yet another forward who never seems to be too far away from the ball in loose play. He is an 'Australian' style of player who is equally happy to have the ball in hand or stifling the ball in a tackle on the opposition. It is felt he is a player to watch on this tour as he could prove to be one of the stars of the trip.

ELWYN GWYTHER Belle Vue Rangers

A Welshman who hails from the Gower Peninsula and was signed from the Llanelli club. He represented a Welsh XV in a 'Victory International before switching to Rugby League with the Manchester outfit in 1947. He quickly established his credentials winning Welsh honours in the new code. While his form this season has not been up there with his best play the selectors were of the opinion that his talents were such, he could not be left out of the touring party. A very strong man in the scrum but like the other props in the party very quick over the ground. He will revel in the hard grounds in Sydney and it is felt will be pushing hard for a spot in the Test team.

HOOKER

FRANK OSMOND Swinton

Yet another Welshman who hails from Newport and went on to play rugby union for that club. He was spotted by the Swinton club who brought him north to play our game in 1948. Since switching codes he has represented his country at international level. He has shown this season that he has that rare talent of never really finishing on the wrong of a scrum count. It this ball winning ability that prompted the selectors to name him in the party. Many feel that he is on a par with Egan when it comes to winning a ball in a scrum. He will be new to the opposition down under and it is felt that he will push Egan hard for a spot in the Test team.

SECOND ROW

DOUG PHILLIPS Belle Vue Rangers

Another Welshman in the tour party, Phillips hails from Neath. While a member of the Swansea club he represented Glamorgan on two occasions before switching codes and joining Oldham in 1945. During the war he had played in a Combined Services game at Bradford and his performance brought him to the attention of rugby league clubs He transferred to the Belle Vue club in 1947 and has gained representative honours for his native Wales. He was a shock selection for the 1946 tour to Australia but his form this season presented the selectors with an easy choice for this tour. This in spite of not playing for Wales in the tour trial. It is felt that his experience will prove invaluable to the less experienced players on the tour.

HARRY MURPHY Wakefield Trinity

Murphy signed for his home town club in 1937 at the age of just seventeen. Since then with a break for the war he has proved to be a good goal kicker when called upon and knows how to score a try as well. He was selected for the tour in 1946 but sadly lasted just twenty minutes before a broken collar bone ruled him out for the rest of that tour. He will be hoping for better luck this time round. He is a no-nonsense player who can be relied upon to provide a consistent performance through out the game. He will enjoy the hard scrummaging work down under.

DANNY NAUGHTON Widnes

Naughton joined the Widnes club during the war years and quickly established himself as a prop in the Widnes mould, tough and uncompromising on the pitch. His play this season for the Widnes club has been such that the selectors placed a close watch on him. The conclusion was that he was the type of forward that would be needed in Australia and New Zealand. The selectors were of the opinion that he would be pushing the more experienced second row forwards for a place in the Test matches.

ROBERT RYAN Warrington

Ryan was born in Wigan and learned the game in that town before being signed by the Warrington club in 1945. Since joining the 'Wires' he has proved a very versatile forward equally at home in the second row and as a loose forward. Earned a place on the tour from his performances in trial games. He has good speed and handles the ball like a three-quarter. Once again a forward who will be well suited to the harder grounds in Sydney and great things are expected from him on the tour.

LOOSE FORWARD

KEN TRAILL Bradford Northern

Born in Northumberland he is the son of the former
player Jim Traill. His selection ahead of Valentine was
very controversial but his performances this season have
made him a stand out loose forward in the game. He
originally joined the Hunslet club but his time there was
interrupted by his National Service. He was signed by
Bradford in 1947 and quickly made the number thirteen
jersey his own. He was selected to play for England
against France earlier in this season and played well in
trial games to cement a place on the tour. He will prove
more than a handful for the opposition down under and
certainly will not take a backward step on the field.

HARRY STREET Dewsbury

Street was spotted playing rugby union as a centre by the St. Helens club and was signed by that club so joining his elder brother Arthur as a member of the professional ranks. In 1949 he was transferred to the Dewsbury club who paid £1,000 for his services. He had by this time switched to the loose forward position and seemed to have found his true position in the game. He gained representative honours with the Yorkshire outfit this season against Wales and France. At twenty three he is still a youngster but great things are expected from him on the tour. The battle between him and Traill for the loose forward spot in the Test team could well be one of the highlights of the tour.

GEORGE OLDROYD Dewsbury Business Manager

Mr Oldroyd is the Chairman of the Dewsbury club and a mill owner in the town. He also has interests in Ireland He is a keen horse racing fan and actually owns a race horse named 'Crown Flats". He is Chairman of the Finance Committee at the Rugby League and has a wealth of experience in the game. He will prove to be a sound business manager for the tour and will continue the traditions of previous tour managers.

TOM SPEDDING Belle Vue Rangers Team Manager

Mr Spedding is very experienced in the entertainment industry previously managing a large hotel on the Isle of Man. He has since taken over the running of the Belle Vue entertainment complex in Manchester. He also is a well known Master of Ceremonies at large boxing matches. He has only sat on Council for a year or so but proved to be both popular and able in his role as Secretary of the Belle Vue Rangers club. Given his experience of dealing with people in the entertainment industry he will prove a popular manager on the tour and it is hoped be instrumental in selecting a team that will retain the Ashes for the Rugby League.

GAMES PLAYED ON TOUR

Date	Opposition	Venue	Result	Gate
May 14	West Aus	Perth	W87-4	7,000
May24	Monaro	Canberra	W37-10	4,600
May 27	Newcastle	Newcastle	W 21-10	22,274
May 31	Riverina	Cootamundra	W 23-13	6,943
June 3	NSW	Sydney	W 20-13	70,419
June 12	Australia	Sydney	W 6-4	47,275
June14	North Coast	Kempsey	W 37-7	7,542
June 17	Queensland	Brisbane	L 15-14	22,118
June 21	North Qld	Townsville	W 39-18	9,500
June 25	Central Qld	Rockhampton	W 88-0	7,000
June28	Wide Bay	Gympie	W 84-9	4,637
July 1	Australia	Brisbane	L 15-3	35,000
July 4	Toowoomba	Toowoomba	W 44-12	7,000
July 6	Brisbane	Brisbane	W 18-8	15,084
July 8	Ipswich	Ipswich	W 18-13	4,946
July12	North Div	Gunnedah	W 41-4	5,313
July 15	NSW	Sydney	W 10-0	24,788
July19	South Div	Wollongong	L 18-11	8,647
July 22	Australia	Sydney	L 5-2	47,187
July 26	South Prov.	Wellington	W 40-15	4,500
July 29	New Zealand	Christchurch	L 16-10	10,000
July 30	West Coast	Graymouth	W 21-15	5,500
Aug. 5	Auckland	Auckland	W 26-17	17,000
Aug. 9	South Auck.	Huntly	W 51-5	4,000
Aug. 12	New Zealand	Auckland	L 20-13	20,000

It should be noted that the Game against Western Districts scheduled for Forbes on the 7th June was actually cancelled and never rearranged.

Printed in Poland
by Amazon Fulfillment
Poland Sp. z o.o., Wrocław

51340500R00120